The Hotel Life of Brian

The Hotel Life of Brian

Brian Wilson

The Book Guild Ltd

First published in Great Britain in 2017 by
The Book Guild Ltd
9 Priory Business Park
Wistow Road, Kibworth
Leicestershire, LE8 0RX
Freephone: 0800 999 2982
www.bookguild.co.uk
Email: info@bookguild.co.uk
Twitter: @bookguild

Illustrations by Faye Thirtle

Typeset in Minion Pro

Printed and bound in Great Britain by CPI Group (UK) Ltd, Croydon, CR0 4YY

ISBN 978 1911320 715

British Library Cataloguing in Publication Data.
A catalogue record for this book is available from the British Library.

To all those volunteers who keep our shores and seas safe for us.

Britain's Independent lifeboats
Royal Lifeboat Institution
National Coastwatch Institution

To Jason
all the Best
Brian W.

Contents

Introduction

The book follows the life of Brian during his twenty-five years in the hospitality industry. The stories recount a number of Brian's bizarre experiences.

Most are hilariously funny, some a bit scary, a few embarrassingly absurd and what is more, they all actually happened.

The tales will cheer you up on a long journey or, if reading in bed, induce a happy night's sleep; as my old gran would say, "Go to sleep with a smile on your face and wake up happy". If you are reading it on a journey, just let the person sitting next to you know it's not them you're giggling at.

I expect, reading my tales, you may be reminded of your own experiences; I bet you will laugh reading mine while recalling your own memories.

Now sit back and enjoy reading this unique collection of short stories, written to make you laugh and see the lighter, funnier side of working in the hospitality industry.

Enjoy reading.

Brian

P.S. Always look on the bright side of life.

Breakfast, American Style

Young trainees are a major source of new lifeblood for every business. They bring fresh ideas and enthusiasm to challenge the baggage, traditions and cultures of some longer-term employees. They sound great, but with them also come rashness, mischief and sometimes gullibility. As a sixteen-year-old college student, I was as gullible as anyone. I knew it all; well, at least I thought I did.

After my first year at college, during the summer vacation, I obtained employment as a waiter in a five-star London hotel and, as early as my second day, my lack of knowledge and experience in dealing with international customers started to get me into trouble.

Tony, the restaurant manager, was always immaculately dressed in a full tail suit and spoke with a somewhat strange Italian accent. I think he was probably a Cockney and this was an act he had used for years. Tony was a strict but very fair man who, from the day I started, instilled in me that 'the customer is always right', and my job was to ensure the guests' every request was to be satisfied, or as he said, "De customer he getsa what he wantsa, OK, Mr Brian?"

Picture the scene: breakfast day two, a busy restaurant, full of wealthy business and tourist customers, most of whom were on the higher side of middle age. So guess my surprise when a young American couple entered and were led by Tony to a table at my station. I guess Tony thought 'small tippers' – give them to the new boy.

I rushed over and greeted them with my normal informal chat about the weather and asked if they had any plans for their stay. They were so eager to tell me they were here as part of their European six-week honeymoon, the places they'd already been and where they were still hoping to go. After the small talk, I presented them with the extensive breakfast menu and left them to decide what they wanted. On my return to the table, the young lady said she couldn't see oatmeal on the menu and she would really like some. "Oh", I said, "In the UK, we call oatmeal *porridge* when it's cooked, and the uncooked oats we call *oatmeal*."

I think it upset her being told this by a mere sixteen-year-old waiter. She just looked up at me and quite sternly said, "I really don't care what you call it, I want a plate of oatmeal!"

I replied in my most servile voice, "Certainly, madam, I suppose you will want hot milk with it?" She abruptly replied, "Of course!"

So down I went to the kitchen store to find the tub of oatmeal. I put some in the bowl, collected a jug of hot milk and took the long walk back across the restaurant to their corner table, unfortunately passing on my way the ever-vigilant Tony. On reaching the table, I presented to the young lady the bowl of dried uncooked oatmeal and offered to mix the hot milk into it.

She looked up at me somewhat astonished and said, "Oh dear, I did expect it to be cooked." I said, "Like porridge?" to which she and her husband, both seeing the funny side, started to giggle.

At this point, Tony arrived, lent over the table and grabbed the plate of oatmeal from in front of the lady, turned to me and shouted, "What de ye thinka we feed here, de chickens?" And before I could reply, the young lady jumped up and shouted back at him, "Hey, penguin, you calling me a chicken? I ordered that because it's what I want, now put it back!" then winked at me and started to eat it.

The next day, we laughed about it and I got the breakfast chef to cook her porridge with heather honey served with fresh cream, and to top it all I got a £10 tip, not bad for serving two breakfasts in 1964.

Lesson learnt: there's a difference between American English and British English.

Flying Fish

As a trainee in the restaurant, I was full of enthusiasm, and I wanted to learn how to carry a large tray on my shoulder, balanced with one hand. It looked so professional. I spent many hours practising at home and at work before I managed to get my hand to bend back far enough to hold the tray level, without spilling any liquid onto it or anything else. My confidence quickly grew over the first weeks.

Friday lunchtimes in the restaurant were always busy, and the most popular dish was the fresh beer-battered fried cod. On this particular Friday, another waiter and I had been taken out of the restaurant to serve a small business party of twelve people in a private dining room on the first floor.

The luncheon started well and, after clearing the starter plates, we went down to the kitchen to collect the main courses. The chef carefully placed three serving dishes on my large tray: one with eight beautifully fried fish, one with chips and one full of peas, alongside two large sauce boats of tartar sauce.

Ever confident, I placed the tray on my shoulder and ran up the stairs. To my surprise, as I turned on the landing, the back of the tray must have just clipped the wall-mounted fuse box. The tray violently flipped forward and catapulted the food across the landing to the facing wall. I remember seeing it in slow motion; the white tartar sauce hitting the wall and the fish sliding down it like skiers, occasionally impeded by the chips and the pea-speckled wall!

In case of any children reading this, I won't repeat what I said, what the chef called me when I went back to ask for replacements for the food adorning the wall, or indeed what he called me every time he saw me for the next week! All I can say is, he was not a happy man, but within minutes, the replacement food was ready, which I carefully carried up the stairs, avoiding the fuse box.

The important fact was, the customers knew nothing about it. They were absolutely delighted with their meal and gave me a large financial tip.

Did I share the party's large financial tip with the chef? Well no, he wouldn't speak to me, but after a few weeks, the chef and I became friends, even if it did cost me a few pints.

First Day in a Hotel Kitchen

I'm not sure if I should have called this story *Great Expectations*, for that was what I had. I was so excited. My mum had my chef's gear spotlessly clean and the hat starched to stand to perfection.

I got an early train to London, then the Underground to the hotel. It was a large old five-star hotel with an impressive private entrance, and a large U-shaped drive, with taxis and limousines parked around it.

With chest out, I walked in through the grand entrance, only to be accosted by a man in uniform, the concierge, asking me, "Can I help you, sir?" I told him I was going to start work in the kitchen, to which he smiled and escorted me back out the front door and round the corner, where he explained that staff must never use the front door. The staff entrance was in the street behind the hotel, so off I went to find this scruffy, poorly painted, double door marked 'Staff and Deliveries', not at all like the impressive front door. Entering, it smelt horrible, even worse as I descended to the sub-basement where I came out into the kitchen.

There were four rows of stoves, each about twenty feet long in this massive room, surrounded by a number of smaller rooms: the pastry room, the butcher's, the fish prep, the cold room, changing room, eating hall and, of course, the chef's office. I was met by a chef de partie, who was in charge of the cold prep area. He showed me where to change and how to get a locker key, after which I went with him to the cold prep area to start work.

The cold prep area was dominated by a huge wooden table. My job for the morning was to make sandwiches for a private party. This involved laying out two hundred slices of bread on the table and buttering them, but not with a knife. I had to warm two pounds of butter until melted, and then liberally paint it on the bread with a four-inch paintbrush. Once I'd buttered the bread, I placed a variety of toppings onto half of the slices, topped them with the remaining bread, stacked them into bundles of ten and trimmed off the edges. These were then wrapped and put onto trays, before being transferred to the cold room for presentation and service in the afternoon.

My afternoon changed very little as the hotel served approximately five hundred afternoon teas, so my butter painting continued. The only difference was the fillings were more varied. Come four o'clock, my day's butter painting was finished and I left, climbing the stairs up to the fresh air.

When I got home, my mother opened my bag. She was amazed and said, "How did you get so much butter on your apron?" I estimated there must have been a pound of solid butter on it and I told her of my disappointment. I had thought I was going to cook, not paint bread all day. I didn't get much sympathy from my mother. All she said was, "Well, someone has to do it, and I hope you did it with pride," To which I replied, "Yes, Mother's Pride."

To add to my disappointment, like all new boys, I was pranked. At my morning break, I went for a cup of tea in the eating hall and whilst collecting it, the staff chef handed me another mug, which said 'head chef' on it and told me to take it to him. I walked across the kitchen and opened the office door to a room accommodating four assistant head chefs and the purchasing officer, and at the far end a door marked 'head chef'. One of the assistant chefs looked over at me and said, "New lad, head chef's through the door." I walked across the room, knocked on the door and entered with mug in hand.

You know that feeling when you twig you've been conned? I had one then. The room was immaculate and the head chef was sitting at a table with a silver tea set in front of him and a bone china cup in his hand. He looked at me and laughed. Very red faced, I turned and left through the outer office, amid a chorus of giggling. When I told my mother, she laughed and said, "Probably not the last time, son."

Cremated

When I was at college, I worked weekends in the kitchen of a large London hotel, mainly in the cold preparation room, but occasionally, I was allowed to cook. I would be given between four and six hundred fillet steaks to cook on the long coke-fuelled ranges.

I would have ten large trays spread out along the range and into each I would very quickly add forty fillet steaks. After that, I would run up and down the range, turning the steaks with what looked like a coal shovel.

Once they were cooked, I would toss them into the storage bin that I dragged along behind me. When they were all cooked, I would rush to the service area where the chefs would prepare them for presentation. Today this would all be done very differently, in a far more controlled and hygienic way.

I really enjoyed working in the kitchen; however I hated the staff food. I imagined it was like what food must have been like on the nineteenth-century war ships, always green looking, smelling of fat with a chewy texture. It was so vastly different to the food we were preparing, cooking and serving to the customers.

Being a tad entrepreneurial, I arranged with other trainees to procure some good food and cook it in the afternoons when nearly all the chefs were off duty. We would then sit down together in the cold prep area and share the food we'd procured, enjoying a good meal. Once we'd procured the food, the problem we often faced was where to keep it, and the answer was in the tall chef's hats we wore. I regularly walked about for an hour or so with a small chicken under my hat, waiting to secure an empty oven to cook it in.

One Saturday afternoon, there were just the three of us trainees in the kitchen. I found a free oven and placed two tiny chickens in to cook for an estimated time of fifteen minutes. As I stood up and turned around, I saw, wandering across the kitchen, the head chef (never before seen in the kitchen on a Saturday afternoon when Chelsea were playing at home). He stood with his back to my oven and didn't move. He simply stood there, looking round the kitchen and making notes on his pad. It was over an hour before he left and another ten minutes before I reckoned the coast was clear.

When I opened the oven door, the birds were as black as charcoal. The head chef had said nothing but I guessed he knew they were in the oven.

Six months later, when I was leaving the hotel for a fulltime job, the head chef called me into his office to wish me well. During the conversation, he told me that one of his most amusing moments had been standing in front of the oven that our chickens were in and wondering if one of us trainees would come for the birds.

I did explain why we did it, in that the food for the kitchen staff was just appalling. He promised to look into it, but I suggested maybe he should try eating it first, which made him laugh.

Some years later, I returned to the same kitchen, which had been totally rebuilt and now had an advanced food preparation facility called a *cook-chill system* in place for banqueting. I was invited to lunch with the staff and, while sitting down with the chefs in the staff canteen, I commented on the quality of the staff food and how different it was to what we were given.

Logical But Wrong

Catering for large numbers, whether it's for functions or factories, brings its moments of mirth and confusion for apprentice chefs as they go through the learning curve.

In this large premier London hotel kitchen, we prepared food for functions with up to nine hundred people. These would vary from simple afternoon teas to nine course dinners, often needing to be cooked under Kosher rules supervised by a Rabbi.

Part of my chef training was working as assistant storekeeper for five days, to learn about the wide variety and quality characteristics of good fresh food and the importance of correct storage.

This is the story of a young trainee chef student called Steve on his work placement from a London College. He was preparing sandwiches for an afternoon party and the egg starter for an evening banquet. The chef had asked him to prepare one of the large boiling pans and cook two hundred hard-boiled eggs.

Steve went rushing off, filling the pan and getting the water ready to introduce the eggs, which he collected from me in the stores. About an hour later, Steve crept back to the store counter and asked if he could have a private word with me, so I came out into the corridor.

Steve: "I don't quite know how the chef expects me to do it?"

Me: "Do what?"

Steve: "Have all those eggs cooked by this afternoon."

Me: "Sorry, Steve, I don't follow you."

Steve: "Well, he asked me to hard-boil two hundred eggs and, as you know, it takes about twelve minutes to hard-boil an egg, so two hundred will take about forty hours!"

Me, with a look of total amazement: "What! How do you work that out?"

Steve: "One egg takes twelve minutes so two hundred multiplied by twelve minutes is forty hours. You know like when we cooked the beef, it was fifteen minutes to the pound so a four pound piece of beef would take an hour?"

Me: "Yes, for a piece of beef because of its thickness and size, but if you put four one-pound pieces of beef in the oven they would take fifteen minutes. You're cooking two hundred individual chicken eggs, not a bloody big ostrich egg two hundred times bigger!"

Steve: "Oh no! What am I going to do? They've been in nearly an hour!"

Me: "Get 'em out and cold as quickly as possible. Put them in the sink and leave the cold water tap running to cool them before they go black."

A lesson well learnt: a little knowledge can get you into a lot of trouble. Steve turned out to be a great chef, but I doubt he will ever forget his boiled eggs lesson.

Lobster Refrain

A young commis chef called Tom was cruelly set up by an experienced chef. His task was to cook twenty-five lobsters in one of the large fixed boiling pans.

A chef colleague of mine spent some time showing Tom how much water to put in the large fixed pan, bringing it up to the right temperature, how to place the lobsters in carefully, and not to worry about the screaming noise as it was just air escaping from the lobster shells. Once the lobsters were in the pot, he left him to cook them with words of caution on the cooking of lobsters.

My first indication of something being wrong was hearing young Tom crying, "I can't stop them, chef, I can't stop them, I've tried, I have!" I ran over to see what was causing him such distress and looked into the pan of part-cooked lobsters with Tom whimpering in my ear.

"They're going red, chef, they're going red!" I quickly explained this is what happens when you cook lobsters, they always go red. Tom looked up at me, still with tears in his eyes and said, "Chef told me to stir them very gently and whatever I did I was not to let them turn red!"

"The b******", I said.

A few minutes later I could see the smile returning to Tom's face as I explained he'd been tricked and just to learn from it, both of us laughed and started to remove the now cooked lobsters.

Once on my own, I laughed at his misfortune, realising it

could have happened to me earlier in my career. Over the next four to five weeks, it was interesting to see how Tom, when asked to do something new to him, would confirm it with someone else before starting. He was a cautious lad.

Sherry Trifle Beware

Beware of what you eat! This is not an incident I was involved in, other than being in the kitchen as a commis chef alongside Pete who was responsible for this act.

It was a normal warm, dry summer's day and Pete, the trainee patisserie chef, was making four large trifles for a lunchtime buffet. After he'd made the sponge bases and placed them in the serving bowls, he soaked them in fruit juice and sherry before covering with crème anglaise.

Then he went to put them in the cold room to cool before adding the cream and fruit topping. But the cold room was jam packed with food, leaving no room for his trifles.

Pete, being ever resourceful, carefully carried them out to the inner quad – a central area within the hotel, open to the elements, where he'd previously cooled food. An hour later, he went to retrieve his trifles, only to discover them covered in dust. He'd forgotten to cover them.

It looked like a lazy chambermaid had emptied a vacuum cleaner bag out of a window and some dust had drifted into his trifles. With only minutes to spare, he hastily scraped off what he could before applying the cream and chocolate topping.

Later, the head chef said that he'd sampled one of the trifles and found the taste interesting but a little gritty, and asked what he had added. Pete told him the first thing he thought of: 'ground nutmeg'. The chef explained nutmeg was not to everyone's taste and not to use it in trifles in future. So, from that day on, no more nutmeg on trifles, or dust, and no more leaving food to cool in the inner quad without covering it first!

Strange, how you can influence a person's taste by telling them what it could be.

Choux Pastry Mountain

Like most chefs, I too have had my share of cooking disasters. One day, the head chef said to me, "Brian, I need something a bit spectacular for the Hogmanay buffet." I replied, "No problem, chef, I'll make a mountain out of profiteroles, a croquembouche but with a difference. I'll build it to be a snow-covered erupting volcano!"

I spent hours planning the finished product. It was to be set in a large tray, four foot by two foot six inches, into which I would put a thin bed of milk chocolate, coated with green coconut to represent grass.

The coconut coating would extend partially up the sides of the mountain, merging into profiteroles coated in dark and milk chocolate representing rocks and, towards the summit, white chocolate signifying snow, with raspberry sauce poured from the top like lava flows.

Finally, for additional effect when I brought it into the restaurant with the lights dimmed, I would ignite hot brandy held in a stainless steel bowl at the top of the mountain and a few sparklers on the side to give it the wow factor.

I constructed the inside and bottom of the mountain with toffee-filled choux balls for strength, then cream-filled choux balls around a triangular chocolate and vanilla sponge as it went up the mountain, to reduce the weight.

I spent days working in the cold room making the mountain, then on 31st December, it was finished and ready for the Hogmanay buffet.

The entrance was truly spectacular: four chefs carried in this erupting volcano, with the guests all standing and clapping. You could hear the wows all round the room and I felt like a king.

Unfortunately, this masterpiece and my feeling of exhilaration didn't last, for within fifteen minutes, all the profiteroles had slid down the mountain into what looked like a huge mud heap in a grassy swamp!

My first mistake was not to realise people were going to destroy it as they took their portion. The second was forgetting that the heat in the restaurant would cause the chocolate to melt quickly. Still, it tasted good!… And for those at the end of the queue, a lovely tasty 'chocolate mess'.

A New Sponge Gateaux Recipe

Everyday was a busy day in the kitchen of this three-star hotel, which had an excellent reputation for fine dining. When on the breakfast/dinner split shift, I started work at 6am, with a long afternoon break, and normally finished about 10pm, except on evenings when there was a function and then it could be midnight before we finished.

I was on breakfast duty with Frank, our university student on work placement at the end of his first year. He was my assistant as the breakfast and pastry cook, as Mrs Wright was on her well-earned annual leave. We were just finishing the breakfast service when the head chef arrived. Seeing the service was coming to an end, he asked Frank to make two sponge gateaux for the lunch service.

A few minutes later, Frank came to tell me there was no self-raising flour in the store. He'd use plain flour and get it to rise by adding baking powder and bicarbonate of soda. I told him we had no baking powder and he'd just have to make the flour grains finer to get the sponges to rise. I told him this was a way not taught in university but the trade way.

Five minutes later, the hotel's general manager Michael made a very unusual and unexpected early morning visit to the kitchen. I shuddered as he walked over to Frank who had 3lbs of plain white flour on the meat chopping board and was laying into it with a meat cleaver. Michael stood to one side of the flour cloud and asked Frank what on earth he was doing, as the flour showered all over him and the kitchen.

Frank explained with great enthusiasm that the chef (me) had told him you can make plain flour rise by simply breaking down the size of the grains. Michael asked, "Is it working, Frank?" Frank took up a handful of flour, passed it through his fingers and said, "Yes sir, I can definitely feel the difference," to which Michael turned and said, "You'd better get on with it then, lad," and left the kitchen.

Ten minutes later, I was summoned to the head chef's office and asked to explain, and we did laugh as I tried to recount what had happened. Thankfully, the head chef and the manager both saw the funny side of it and no further action was taken. Later, even Frank took it in his stride, seeing the funny side of it, and a year later, got his own back when he caught out a new student on their work placement with another induction prank.

Specialist Cooking Pans

Frank our university student, returned a year later to work in the kitchen, but this time a little wiser, more mature and a much more confident young man.

Shortly after his arrival, we had a buffet which included dressed salmons for 250 people. Frank was allocated the task of preparing, cooling and decorating them with the help of that year's new student, Peter. They did a great job. The three salmons were poached to perfection in the salmon kettles, then dressed and beautifully presented on silver salvers, with many of the guests commenting on their excellence.

A week later, we were to prepare the annual buffet lunch for a local fishing club and the host had asked if we could provide 'collared eel'; an old-fashioned dish where the eel is cooked whole and served in its own cooking pot and liqueur. Frank and I had cooked this dish the previous year for the same customer, so I asked Frank to prepare and cook it, and have Peter assist him as part of Peter's training. Later that day, I saw Frank sitting down with Peter, producing a work plan for the banquet.

Three days after asking Frank to prepare the collared eel, the hotel receptionist transferred a phone call to me from the manager of our main catering supplier in Cheltenham. He told me one of our young chefs had called into the shop to ask if they could procure a twenty-inch S-shaped eel skillet pan but unfortunately he was having difficulty in finding a supplier of this kind of pan. I told him not to worry, that as time was now short we would manage with what we had and I would call him back later if I needed one.

I called Frank and asked him to explain what this was all about. He told me he had convinced Peter that after cooking the salmon in a salmon kettle; he would need a specialist pan to cook eels, an 'eel skillet pan'.

Frank had described an eel skillet pan as approximately twenty-four inches long and S-shaped to fit the whole eel in for cooking and service. He then sent Peter into Cheltenham on his day off to find one. It appears that Peter was not the only one convinced of the existence of an S-shaped eel skillet pan, as the next day, I received calls from two more suppliers regretting they were unable to source a supplier.

I will point out to the best of my knowledge that there is no such thing as an S-shaped, two-foot skillet pan. At the time, the only one not amused was Peter as he'd spent most of his day off going round suppliers convincing them there was such a pan. But within a week, he was laughing about it and trying to find a way to get back at Frank.

A Problem with the Gas

Margaret, a young local girl, had been working with her sisters and mother as a casual in housekeeping during her school holidays and weekends for some time. Now having left school, she had just started full-time employment as a trainee manager in her first department, the restaurant.

The story starts as the dinner service was nearing the end. It had been a busy night but now there were just a few customers left to be served their main and dessert courses, including a party of six regular customers who, unfortunately, had arrived nearly an hour later than booked. Being late had caused a slight bottleneck in the kitchen, resulting in a short delay in this party receiving their main course.

After waiting a couple of minutes, a lady from this party beckoned Margaret over to the table and asked if their main course could be hurried up as she had a babysitter to get back home for. Margaret rushed into the kitchen and up to the hotplate, where she gabbled, "Chef, chef, table three are getting a bit upset waiting for their main course – is it ready yet – table four had theirs five minutes ago?"

Chef told her to calm down and said it would be ready in a couple of minutes. He went on to explain there was a problem with the gas pressure, and perhaps she could help speed things up by going to reception and getting a couple of shillings to put in the gas meter. She looked at him totally perplexed. "A place like this has a gas meter?" she asked. "Yes, you know how mean Michael is," he replied, to which she replied, "Okay then."

Chef handed her a petty cash slip for five shillings. As she left the kitchen he phoned Jane on reception to let her in on the prank, and asked one of the waiters to come and collect the meals now ready for table three.

Unbeknown to us at the time, Jane gave Margaret the five single coins and the cellar keys, and directed her to the paint store in the cellar, where she would find the gas meter situated next to twelve large cans of tartan paint. Margaret was in the paint store for a few minutes before realising she had been tricked.

In the meantime, the customers (regulars) had started their main course and been told of the little prank being played on their new waitress. On her return to the restaurant, the regulars all applauded and before leaving the table, gave Margaret a big tip, either because they felt sorry for her or because they hadn't laughed so much in a long time. They told her it was for being so helpful and cheerful in what were difficult circumstances, so all's well that ends well. The next day, Margaret and her family popped into the kitchen shook their fists at the chef then burst out laughing.

Summer Punting

Working in a small Cotswold town with a group of male trainees was great and lots of fun, especially on days when we met up with the female trainees from the nearby hotel in Moreton-in-Marsh.

On sunny summer days, we would go punting on the Thames at Lechlade. We'd all pile into a couple of cars and drive down to Lechlade. From the high street, we would turn right over the hump-backed bridge, drive about a hundred yards, then right again into the car park field.

We would park the cars. Then two of us lads would change and swim across the river to collect a couple of punts and come back with them. We'd pick up the rest of the group and go off up river for a picnic lunch. Then we'd race back, drop off the punts and be in time for a drink in the pub. This was one of those days.

Timothy, our six foot four inches tall trainee, had purchased a nearly new Mini and boy, was he proud of it. He even called her Mima. The day had started with a light rain shower and then the sun came out, as twenty-two of us set off from Cirencester in four cars to spend a day on the river. Yes, we were rather packed into the cars; in fact Timothy had six in his Mini! As we entered the car park field, Timothy shouted, "The last person to the other side pays for the punts!"

At this point, he accelerated his Mini across the field, braking about thirty yards from the riverbank. Unluckily for him, the grass was still slightly wet from the early morning shower and with the brakes on, the car majestically skated across the field and slid slowly over the riverbank into two feet of water!

We rushed over, taking care not to follow Timothy into the river, and helped everyone out of the partially submerged Mini and onto the riverbank. Everyone, including Timothy, was in fits of laughter, some of which was down to shock, but also the huge relief at being able to get out of the car and only be waist-deep in water.

Needless to say, punting was abandoned for the day. I won't say it completely spoiled our trip out. Eating our picnic on the riverbank beside the partially submerged Mini, we watched the tractor carefully pull it out of the river onto the garage recovery vehicle, under the watchful eye of the local constabulary. They were not happy and gave Timothy a right telling off with a note to report to the local police station with his licence and the car's documents.

Five days later Timothy came to see me, almost in tears. The garage had just called him to say the car was fixed but there was a problem in that the car was a cut and shunt. Ignorant to this phrase, I asked what it meant. He explained the front half of his precious Mima was an Austin and it had been welded to the back half of a Morris! What was worse, the Police had told him he would have to pay for the car to be fully inspected to make sure it was safe before they would let it back on the road.

The good news is we had a whip round, so Mima and Timothy were soon reunited to spend the rest of the year touring all over Gloucestershire, but needless to say, far away from water!

Spooks

As a night porter, either working on your own or as part of a team, you see the world differently from the daytime workers. Working in the dark tends to be quieter and at night, normal noises can have a spooky effect on you. Added to this, people you deal with at night often behave quite differently to the way they do during the day. Some have had far too much to drink, some are half asleep and grumpy and a few have criminal intent but the majority are a pleasure to deal with. All this makes the job interesting but requires a special, calm type of person.

Like all very old buildings, this three-hundred-plus-year-old hotel had its ghost and the stories told were of a spectral Royalist soldier who always appeared if the 'Confessor's Chair' was moved. This chair was a very heavy, large, old oak carved chair. It stood at the foot of the main staircase beside the cellar door and was occasionally moved by the day staff to clean under and behind it.

On this particular night, I'd been out late with friends and was approaching the hotel just after 2am when the front door flew open and out ran Frank, our new part-time night porter, in obvious distress. I ran up and stopped him to find out what was wrong but he kept saying, "I know I shouldn't have moved the bloody Confessor's Chair, I disturbed him, I did! I'm not going back, I'm off!" as he thrust the hotel keys into my hand and ran off down the road, leaving me to enter on my own.

In his haste to leave, he'd switched off all the entrance hall lights. I entered apprehensively in the dark, feeling my way along the wall to the light switch. With the lights now on, I felt much braver and made my way to the stairs, where I noticed the Confessor's Chair had been moved. It was no longer in its usual position but was now sitting up against the cellar door, with the vacuum cleaner still plugged in beside it. It seems Frank had moved the chair to vacuum under it, a job superstitiously always done by the day staff.

I put the vacuum cleaner away in the cupboard and set about moving the rather heavy chair back to its normal position when I heard the noise of somebody coming down the stairs. I stepped back to let them pass but there was no one there. In shock, I stepped back and stumbled into the cellar door, which suddenly burst open, giving me the fright of my life. This left me wishing I had just left the chair where it was and gone straight to my room.

For a second, I just stood there, frozen to the spot and shaking with terror, when a cold hand suddenly touched mine.

I gasped! With my eyes tightly shut so as not to see the hotel ghost, I heard a voice say, "Thank god you moved that bloody chair. I've been trying to get out of the cellar for the last hour! I've been shouting and banging the underside of the stairs but no one heard me, and you've no idea how spooky it is in the cellar when you can't get out!" The voice sounded familiar so I turned my head and, to my pure relief, I saw Nigel the barman standing there.

As my colour and power of speech returned, we sat down and he told me what had happened. As he was off work for the next couple of days, he'd decided to help by tidying up the cellar, ready for the draymen in the morning. So, after finishing at the late function in the ballroom, he'd come down to tidy the cellar but while working in there, someone must have put the Confessor's Chair in front of the door.

He'd tried pushing the door but it wouldn't budge and he knew banging on it wouldn't be heard on the other side because the inside of the door was highly padded for heat insulation. So to draw attention to his captivity, he'd been banging on the stairs with the brush every few minutes.

What he didn't realise was, it sounded like someone coming down the stairs and had frightened the life out of poor Frank and me.

I did enjoy phoning Frank in the morning to tell him all about his ghost, but I omitted telling him exactly how frightened I'd been!

The Lost Bite

I remember one morning being called to the restaurant by Margaret, our trainee, to help her deal with a gentleman who was raging at her. She had no idea why. All she could understand was that he couldn't eat the breakfast in front of him. He'd ordered scrambled eggs, tomato and a sausage. A couple of minutes after placing the food in front of him, she returned to ask if everything was to his satisfaction. It was then he appeared to get upset, waving his arms around.

As I approached the gentleman, his head disappeared under the table followed by the rest of his body. A few moments later, he resurfaced on the other side with a huge smile as he popped his false teeth back into his mouth. He'd taken them out and forgotten where they were. They must have fallen off the table. I think it was the embarrassment of losing his teeth that was causing him such concern. Later Margaret said he was so nice and apologetic to her.

It reminded me of when I was a child. My dad every Christmas made shortbread rounds for all his family and friends. He told me that the finger twist edging on the rounds he did with his false teeth. I was twelve before realising it was his finger and thumb.

Half Pint Regulars

On weekday mornings at 11am, when the hotel lounge bar opened, its first customers were usually four old boys and two dogs, commonly known as the 'last of the summer wine boys'. They'd come in for about an hour, sit in front of the fire and work out their daily four shilling bet, while each having a half pint of beer and one for the dogs.

In the first fifteen minutes, Peter the barman completed the cleaning, including mopping the floor and washing the odd glass or two from the night before. After that, he'd sit on a stool behind the bar to read the paper or have a wee nap, often forgetting to turn off the sink tap.

On these occasions, the old boys would have an additional bet amongst themselves as to:

a) How far the water would go before Peter woke up?
b) Would it make the twenty feet to the door?
c) Or would the manager come in and wake him up?

But one thing they never bet on was the calamity that followed.

Roger, one of the trainee managers, walked in with a bucket of sludgy beer, slipped on the wet floor, then, trying to keep his balance, grabbed the bar counter.

In doing so, the beer bucket went flying through the air, landing neatly upside down on Pete's lap, causing him to jump up, crash into the shelf above and sends a bottle of Scotland's finest malt whisky in the direction of the four old boys!

Picture the chaos: four old boys flying off their seats like lightning with eight hands shooting into the air, desperate to grab the bottle of nectar malt, while their dogs legged it across the room to get as far away from the commotion as possible.

Well, they missed the bottle, which hit the fireplace mantelshelf, smashing on impact and covering all four of them in malt whisky!

They didn't grumble. Instead, they got a taste of fine malt whisky for free, but not Peter, who had to pay for the replacement.

Changing the Barrel

The beer cellar in the hotel was directly under the public bar. Changing a barrel required one to exit the bar, walk down the arcade, enter the hotel lobby, cross the reception hall, unlock the cellar, go down the narrow staircase and walk thirty yards back along the low narrow passage to the beer cellar.

It was a wet winter's morning and the bar had been open for less than an hour. The 'last of the summer wine boys' were, as usual, sitting by the fire sorting out their daily bet over a beer.

Peter had just finished his morning cleaning and was about to take up his position on a bar side stool when a stranger arrived, walked up to the far end of the bar where Pete had just deposited himself, and ordered a pint of Guinness.

Peter reluctantly got off his stool, huffed and walked round the bar. He was half way through pouring the pint when the tap started blowing air. The cask was empty. Peter swore under his breath, ran out of the bar heading for the cellar to change the barrel. A couple of minutes later Guinness started to flow from the beer tap which Pete had left on.

After filling the pint glass, the Guinness started overflowing into the beer tray then cascaded down onto the floor, at which point one of the old boys walked over and turned the tap off. He finished pouring the customer his pint then said to the stranger, "He's probably forgotten what he went for; just pay Peter when he gets back." Five minutes later still no Peter, so another of the old boys walked across to reception and asked if they knew where

Peter was, as he had gone to change a barrel some time ago and hadn't come back, and there were now customers waiting in the bar.

I received a call from reception telling me of the scenario, and went down to the cellar to investigate. I found poor Peter unconscious, lying on his back in the cellar corridor, and quickly called for an ambulance. Later that day, I went to the hospital to collect Pete and find out what had happened. He told me it was as he had connected the beer pipe to the new Guinness tank, he remembered he'd left the beer tap turned on in the bar and ran at full speed down the corridor, only to meet one of the low ceiling beams on the way, where he came to an acute stop as it impacted on his forehead, and boy, what an impression that left!

Two days later, Peter was back at the bar showing off his very impressive bulging blue forehead and, as a thanks to his old pals for getting him help, he bought them each a beer. While he held court, telling them of the erotic dreams he had while unconscious on the cellar floor.

Big Louis

In my time, I've employed many temporary chefs, some very good and a few dreadful. However, big Louis was one of the good guys. He was a very talented chef, six foot five inches in height and just over twenty stone, what one would call a larger than life character.

This story happened at the time when the James Bond film *The Man with the Golden Gun* was the big box office hit.

At the time, I lived in the hotel staff house, along with about twenty other workers. On the ground floor of the house there was a large living room with TV, kitchen, toilet and laundry. The two floors above were divided into small single rooms, with a bathroom and separate toilet on each floor. At this time, showers in bathrooms were unheard of and people had a bath once a week, whether they needed it or not. Showers, well, they were for when you came out of the swimming pool.

Louis was, as I've said, a big strong lad, and I remember him lifting Nigel's car engine out of the Mini for him. Nigel had a bad habit of when he heard someone in the bathroom, he would kick the door, and, because of the temporary nature of the structure, the door would sometimes fly open. Nigel would then poke his head round the open door and wish good day to whoever was in the bath. It mattered not if they were male or female, though normally on our floor, it would be one of the guys.

On this particular Sunday afternoon, Nigel heard someone in the bathroom. So, as was his wont, he kicked the door, which subsequently flew open, but unfortunately, big Louis was on the other side getting out of the bath. The doorknob hit him on the bum, sending him naked into his half-filled bath!

On hearing the shouts and seeing it was big Louis, Nigel took fright and rushed down the first floor corridor to his room, where he locked himself in. However, he was closely followed by a naked, raging six-foot-five Louis, who banged his door so hard that the whole wall moved.

At this point, Nigel was screaming apologies to Louis and, in fear for his life, jumped out of the first floor window and ran off down the road, not to be seen till the next day at work. Hearing the commotion, I went upstairs and met Louis as he was returning to the bathroom, vowing to kill that stupid prat. After a cup of tea, he calmed down but made it clear he was going to sort that Nigel out.

The following day, Nigel, who was working in the bar, walked into the kitchen, making sure the hotplate was between him and Louis. Here he spent a good ten minutes apologising and grovelling to Louis, who had by this time calmed down, but the big man told him he would bide his time to get his own back.

Louis's Revenge

A few weeks after Nigel's unfortunate incident, Louis arrived back at the house to watch the Saturday football match on the television. On looking round the room, he asked where Nigel was. Someone said they thought he was having a bath. Louis quietly left, made his way up to his room and down the corridor to the bathroom, where he stopped, listened, and then pushed the door open to see Nigel lying there in the bath.

Seeing Louis, Nigel jumped up and stood there petrified and screaming, trying to hide his privates. Louis grabbed his arm, spun him round, and sprayed his bum with silver paint.

Once he had finished, Louis calmly turned, walked down the stairs and out of the house, leaving Nigel screaming at him from the landing.

We rushed up from the TV room to find Nigel stark naked, trying to look over his shoulder at his silver bottom. All we could do was curl up and laugh while Nigel ran into his room and shut the door, still screaming obscenities and ranting that it wasn't funny having a silver bum. It looked like two silver salvers!

About ten minutes later, Nigel poked his head round the door of the TV room and asked if Gordon and I would come up to his room. On our arrival, he told us that he'd tried to take the paint off with white spirit, but now his buttocks were really burning. We could see the silver had a definite red glow to it.

A group decision was taken and off to A&E we went, with Nigel in the back of the car. Checking in at the hospital was embarrassing, as you can imagine. Needless to say they cleaned him up and discharged him, but on his way out, the reception nurse said it had been a day to remember as she had seen *The Man with the Golden Gun* the night before and 'the man with the silver bum today'.

The Bunker Boys

This story centres on two young trainees at a beautiful country hotel with an adjoining eighteen-hole golf course, and their car, purchased for £50, a Citroën DS1, which to say the least was in need of some, no, lots of tender loving care.

It was a Saturday morning and I was duty manager, when at 6am I was woken by the hotel's golf course head greenkeeper, phoning to tell me some idiot had left a car in the bunker halfway up the 10th fairway. The car had the ignition keys in it and an up-to-date hotel car park pass on the windscreen, but, as he said, "The car did not appear to be the type any of our well-heeled residents would own."

He asked what he should do: call the police or move it. Not fully awake, I told him to get it off the golf course, but not to phone the police until he heard from me. I asked what type of car it was and if he knew who owned it. All he knew was that it was a rather tatty old Citroën and he would need the tractor to tow it back to the clubhouse.

In my sleepy state, I was thinking the car may have been taken from the car park for a joy ride. Now wide awake, I dressed and went off to talk to Gordon, the head night porter, to find out if he knew anything about it.

Gordon told me he'd overheard two of our management trainees talking about buying a Citroën. I rushed down the corridor to the trainees' rooms, where I found Nigel and James in the land of bliss, sound asleep and absolutely reeking of booze. I woke them none too gently to ask about their car. They confirmed they had just bought a Citroën and assured me it was in the staff car park. I told them to get up and check, then report to me in my office.

An hour later, they arrived at my office to tell me their car was not in the car park and it must have been stolen. After more thorough questioning, they concurred that they couldn't remember exactly where they'd parked it. I suggested calling the police to report it missing, at which a look of grave concern came over their faces and they started to explain what really happened.

They'd bought the car the day before and had been out with friends, ending up at the golf pro's house on the far side of the golf course, where they partied till the early hours. I asked how they'd got home. They warily explained it had been foggy and, being a bit intoxicated, they'd taken the tractor path across the golf course, but couldn't actually remember putting the car in the car park. In fact, their last memory before I woke them in their room was deciding to sleep in the car.

I asked them to wait while I went into the next office to discuss the episode with my boss, the hotel owner. On telling him the story, he smiled and burst out laughing. He told me that, as a youngster, he'd often driven home across the golf course to avoid the police, but never managed to bunker himself.

His decision was to get his police pal in to give them an unofficial warning, while he would think of a suitable punishment. I returned to my office and told them the police were on their way to interview them. In the meantime, they were to wait in the car park for the police to arrive.

Two hours later, with them still freezing in the car park, the hotel owner went out with his friendly policeman. The policeman gave them a real dressing down, emphasising that they could be charged with criminal damage and it was only by the good grace of the owner they were not being charged.

Then the boss told them where the car was, and what their punishment was. It was five days of raking the golf course bunkers before work, starting at 5.30am the next day. I know they were relieved at the leniency of the punishment. After this incident, they became known as 'the bunker boys'.

DIY Car Repairs

The 'bunker boys' kept the car for a few months, until one spring evening, when they phoned to ask if I could pick them up. They explained they'd had a small accident and although they and the car were okay, it was not drivable. As they were only about a mile away, they wanted to know if I could possibly come over in the Land Rover and tow their car back to the car park.

Well, it wasn't too far and I was off duty, so I picked up one of the estate Land Rovers to bring them and the vehicle back to the garage.

I arrived to find their car rather banged up and randomly parked in the front garden of a lady's semi-detached house. The damage to the car was a bit more than I was led to believe, with both front wings bashed and a caved-in front grill, but thankfully the damage to the property was limited to the garden.

It appeared that on turning left off the main road, they'd careered up the adjoining house's driveway, crossed their front garden and driven through the dividing fence, coming to rest on the lady's front lawn.

When I arrived, the boys were explaining to the lady and her neighbour why they didn't want to go through their insurance company, but would pay for the fence and put the gardens straight themselves. I think the owners took pity on them, because they agreed, and the lads, true to their promise, completed the repairs within a week.

Once back at the hotel, I asked the boys what on earth had

happened. *I mean, how do you go in one driveway and try to exit from another?* Out came the story…

The car had broken down about an hour earlier, a mile or so down the road from the accident. The accelerator cable had snapped, so to get home, they tied a piece of string to the accelerator spring fitted on the carburettor in the engine. From there, the string came out of the side of the bonnet, round the wing mirror, then through the driver's small front quarter light window.

Nigel had the other end of the string tied to his finger. Easy: pull the string and the car goes faster, release it and the car slows down. The movement of the string required for this to happen is minimal. Before setting off home, they tested it a couple of times, accelerating then decelerating.

It all went well for the first few minutes, until turning a very tight left-hand corner required Nigel to put both hands on the steering wheel. Now, with both hands on the steering wheel including the one holding the string, his troubles started.

As he concentrated on turning the corner, he was actually tugging the string, resulting in the car accelerating at great speed. It sped up the driveway of the first house, at which point, Nigel let go of the steering wheel and slammed on the brakes, but the car continued on, skidded across the garden and through the fence, before coming to rest on the neighbour's lawn.

What did the boys learn? When you turn the steering wheel anticlockwise, your hands move away from the window, and if your finger is attached to a piece of string tied to the accelerator, the result will be rapid car acceleration and total loss of control of the vehicle!

The next day, they wisely decided to have the car lifted for scrap before it got them into further trouble.

Morning Call, Sir

I remember Colin with great affection. He was a night porter in the hotel. He was always cheerful, willing and totally dedicated to ensuring customers got the best service possible. It was just unfortunate he sometimes got things wrong.

He was nicknamed 'Sergeant Major Chaos' because of his habit of standing to attention with his chest pumped out and saluting when saying thank you or goodbye to customers.

The hotel was used as a training venue for a large international company, hosting about thirty weekly conferences a year for its senior executives from all over the world. Because of the amount of business they had in the hotel, there was a resident senior trainer, Mr Wright, who also acted as the company's conference liaison officer, an excellent host to his guests and a perfectionist in ensuring each delegate's needs were fully met.

I often had dinner with Mr Wright on the nights when there were no resident delegates and it's from him this story came.

Mr Wright's background to the event:

It happened during the June international conference for vice presidents, one of the highlights of the company year. The conference involved around fifty senior officials arriving from all over the world on the Sunday afternoon and evening in time for the conference start after breakfast on the Monday morning.

The story started to unfold on the Tuesday morning, during a session I was delivering on corporate ethics. I was being completely distracted by Jake, a six foot four inch tall Canadian vice president, sitting at the front. He would start smiling, leading to spasms of quiet giggling, which I was finding more and more difficult to ignore. In the end, I stopped my presentation and said to Jake, "There's obviously something you're finding extremely funny. Perhaps you'd like to share the joke with the rest of us?"

This is what Jake had to say:

Following a twelve-hour journey, I arrived here at the hotel on Sunday, just after midnight, and I was absolutely exhausted. I had a quick sandwich and a glass of beer with the guys who were still in the bar before retiring to my room, which I must say is fantastic. It's a large south-facing room with a huge curtained window, while the other three walls, including the doors, are all light wood panelled.

Being in a strange bed, I had a somewhat restless night. At about 6.30am, yesterday morning I heard the door open. The main light in the room went on and someone marched into the room, clattering a tray down on the bedside table. The person then walked over to the window, opened all the curtains, letting in pure bright sunlight, before turning to the bed and, in a very loud regimental voice, wished me a very hearty "Good morning, sir." Standing to attention, he then turned and exited the room, leaving me in a complete state of shock from the loud awakening, and totally blinded by the bright morning sun directly beaming at me through the huge window.

After slowly waking, bathing and dressing, I went down and found the man standing behind the porter's desk. I leant over the desk, put my face right next to his and said, "Don't you dare wake me like that tomorrow! Just come in quietly, leave the light off, the curtains closed and very quietly say, 'Good morning, Mr Bates', then leave, shutting the door as quietly as possible behind you. I'll then wake up in my own time and in a good way, not like today." The guy apologised profusely to me and promised to be much quieter in future.

Well, this morning, I heard the door open and, true to his word, he crept across the room in the dark, put the tray down and whispered rather timidly, "Good morning, Mr Bates, it's just after 6.30, sir," and left the room.

I was slowly coming to when I heard knocking on a door. Wondering what it was, I turned on the bedside lamp and heard, "I say, sir, please could you open the door?" Still half asleep, I got up and opened the bedroom door to find no-one outside, just an empty corridor. I then heard the knock again, but this time I recognised it was from inside the room. I walked over to the large built-in wardrobe and opened the door to find in it, standing to attention, the night porter!

He smiled and very formally said, "Thank you very much, sir," saluted and marched out of the room, leaving me standing there in my jamas totally dumbfounded.

Back to Mr Wright:

By this time, the whole group were in total hysteria at Jake's waking experience, especially when I told them the porter was affectionately known as Sergeant Major Chaos.

Finally, Jake told me he made sure the bedroom nightlight was on the next morning and for the rest of his stay.

Early Breakfast

Because of the international nature of our conferences, guests would arrive and leave at various times throughout the day and night. Those leaving very early in the morning, before the restaurant opened, would be offered a cooked breakfast. This would be prepared and served by the night porters, either in the guest's room or in the small lounge.

The last night of conference was often rather late and sometimes a boozy event in the private lounge, going on till the early hours. This story is as spoken by Mr Wright, the conference liaison officer, while we were having breakfast.

Mr Wright's story

There's one breakfast I'll always remember. It was on a departure day after a late night socialising with my colleagues from across Europe. I was awoken just before 5am by Sergeant Major Chaos coming into the room, turning on all the lights and placing a tray on the over-bed table.

When I looked at him, in my very sleepy state, he smiled and, in his normal military style, said, "Good morning, sir, here's your breakfast," then proceeded to help me sit up! At this point I mumbled, "I ordered no breakfast and I don't want one."

His reply was, "Now, don't be silly, sir, I've cooked this breakfast just for you so come along now, sit up and eat it all," as he placed the table onto the bed and poured coffee into my cup. Not being fully awake or *compos mentis*, and feeling he was going to stand there until I started to eat, I made a start on the scrambled eggs and thankfully he left.

Just as I was finishing the breakfast, the door flew open and there stood Sergeant Major Chaos. He was looking very forlorn and in a pitiful voice said, "Oh sir, you didn't eat that breakfast did you?" to which I replied, "Yes I bloody well did." "But it wasn't yours," he stammered, "it was for next door." I somewhat angrily told him, "I didn't ask for the b***** breakfast you brought me so b***** off," and he rushed out the door, full of apologies for upsetting me.

Mr Wright continued...

It was later that morning I learned from Gordon, the head night porter, what happened. Two of our conference delegates had ordered 5am breakfasts in their rooms, before catching the hotel chauffeur-driven limousine to Gatwick Airport. Gordon had given Sergeant Major Chaos the order for him to prepare and deliver one full English breakfast to room 315, and scrambled egg with bacon to room 316.

Fifteen minutes later, Chaos had arrived back at the desk announcing 'mission accomplished', but at 5.25am, room 316 telephoned the desk to ask where his breakfast was. Chaos explained to Gordon that he'd taken both trays up, delivered the first to room 315, then next door to deliver mine. Evidently at this point Gordon exploded, calling him an idiot and reminding him 317 was my room. After which Gordon said Chaos ran back to my room to retrieve the breakfast that I'd just eaten.

It appeared Sergeant Major Chaos forgot that room numbers, like houses in streets, are numbered even on one side and odd on the other side of the corridor."

And back to me

When Mr Wright had completed his tale, I asked him if he'd

complained at the time. He said, "No, later in the morning, I did speak to Gordon about it and he told me the gentleman in room 316 had settled for a takeaway bacon sandwich and coffee to eat in the limousine on the way to the airport, and me, well I went back to sleep with a full stomach."

Beer Boobs

This relates to a rather unusual group of gentlemen who, for about six months, came to the hotel every weekend. In the beginning, their bills were paid in cash. However they soon presented bank credit details and went on to monthly payment terms. Initially, payments were on time but, after the third month, payments stopped. Finally, one weekend, while they were out playing golf, we confiscated their luggage, agreeing to return it only on payment of their outstanding account. They were quick to point out it was Sunday and they wouldn't be able to pay until the next day. The owner was adamant – no payment, no luggage, so they left without their things to come back and settle the account the next day. They never did collect the luggage, pay the outstanding bill, or return to the hotel.

As stated, they were an unusual group for this rather old fashioned luxury style of hotel. They always turned up in Rolls Royces and were listed as directors of a company. In reality, we later found out they were also the chauffeurs. They would arrive on a Friday evening, spend a lot of money and leave late on the Sunday afternoon. In general, they were well behaved, kept to themselves and very generous in tipping the staff. My first encounter with them was one Friday evening. Just after they had arrived, I received a call from a suite to replace a bedside light.

I arrived at the room, occupied by one of the young directors and his lady friend, to replace the lightbulb. Once it was replaced and checked, I turned to the couple and asked if there was anything else. The man said, “No, that’s fine,” and turned to the young lady, saying, “Go on, give him a tip.” Her response was to lift up her jumper and push out her ample bare breasts, at which the gentleman said, “Well lad, what do you think of these?” Somewhat confused and embarrassed, I replied, “They won’t buy me a beer,” and left the room with them giggling in the background.

A couple of years later I met them in a pub at Shepherds Market London. She, remembering our last encounter, offered to get me a beer, walked over to the barman ordered the beer and when told the price pulled up her jumper and said, “Take it out of these.” Well everyone in the pub laughed and the barman said, “OK, but there will be no change.”

After Dinner Cabaret

I recall it was a cold winter's Saturday night, the hotel's accommodation was full and a large function was using all of the ground floor public areas, including the lounge bar area at the foot of the main staircase. It was crowded with guests in formal evening attire, enjoying a break from the rigours of dancing or just having a quiet chat after dinner.

This particular guest, whose name I forget, but let's call him George, arrived about 10pm. As by this time the restaurant was closed, he went straight to his room, where he ordered a meal with a half bottle of wine from room service. Having enjoyed his meal in his bedroom, he placed the used tray outside his bedroom door to be collected, and prepared to retire for the night.

This is how the story unfolds, as told by George when we met for coffee before his departure the next day.

George's story

Sleep was not coming quickly and, after about fifteen minutes, I sleepily got up to go to the toilet. I stepped through the door and, as it gently shut behind me, I thought, *Damn!* I'd opened the wrong door and instead of standing in the bathroom, I was in the corridor. It got worse… I was totally naked! It was just like being in a nightmare but I was very much awake and in a hotel corridor stark naked. What could I do?

I was locked out: had no key, no clothes, no phone, nothing.

I glanced up the long corridor and, to my relief, there was no one there, thank goodness, but unfortunately no phones either. I looked down and saw the dinner tray was still where I had left it. I picked up the large white cloth serviette and held it in front of me for modesty, as I slowly walked along the corridor looking for a phone to contact a member of staff to let me back into my room.

I couldn't find a phone or a member of staff, but I could hear voices coming from the staircase at the end of the corridor. On reaching the staircase, I kept my back to the wall and peered through the banister. I could see the lounge bar staff, who fortunately were facing my way, but serving customers and totally unaware of my presence or predicament, as were the sixty to seventy people sitting at the bottom of the stairs in the lounge area.

I had to get the attention of the bar staff, so holding the serviette in place with one hand and waving with the other, I started to slowly creep down the staircase, keeping my back as close to the wall as possible.

It was amazing, just like a football stadium 'Mexican Wave'. The silence spread across the lounge seating area as people became aware of me on the stairs and turned to look. Suddenly one of the bar staff ran out from behind the bar and made for the staircase, at which point I smiled to the people below and turned to ascend the stairs to the safety of my room.

I suddenly remembered that the serviette was only covering my front and now my bum was in full view, so I quickly pulled the serviette round to cover my rear, at which point the crowd below broke out into spontaneous applause. I had never felt so embarrassed, but you know the amazing thing is, at breakfast this morning, nobody recognised me, with my clothes on!

After telling me his unfortunate tale, he wished me well and left saying he would be back, but next time he would make sure it was the bathroom he went into naked before shutting the door.

A Dog with Taste

It was a sunny, summer Saturday afternoon and the wedding party had just finished their meal. The speeches were in full flow when one of my fellow trainee managers came to tell me I was wanted at reception.

On my arrival, Mr C, the hotel owner, who was a jolly, podgy middle-aged gentleman, told me one of his dogs, a large brown Labrador named Bongo, must have gone for a wander and a lady in the nearby village had just phoned to say the dog was in her house!

"I would very much appreciate it if you would go down to the garage, collect a car and pick him up," he said as he handed me the address. Bongo was a big placid dog who spent much of his time wandering round our office, so to pick him up seemed like no problem.

Off I went down to the hotel garage where the hotel kept a small fleet of vehicles, including three limousines used for picking up and transporting guests, one red Rolls Royce, a blue Bentley convertible, a Black Maria, two Land Rovers, a small Austin Princess and two smaller vans.

At the garage, I was met by a new chauffeur on his first weekend duty. I told him I needed a vehicle to go and pick up Bongo, the owner's dog. He looked round the garage and said, "Take the Black Maria, it's just by the door." I picked up the keys and headed off in the large black van down to the village two miles away.

On arrival at the lady's house, she explained that they'd seen the dog lying on their front lawn and went out to see if it was all right. When they reached the dog, it rose up, turned, walked through their open door into the house and lay down by the fireplace, where it had stayed placid but refusing to move.

On entering the room, I said, "Come on, Bongo." To the family's amazement, the dog slowly arose and sauntered out to the van with me. However, when I opened the back door of the van, the dog turned and sauntered back into the house, returning to its place by the fire.

I pulled, shouted and even tried to lift him, but he was staying. I borrowed the lady's telephone (no mobiles in those days), phoned Mr C and explained what had happened. I was not expecting the mouthful I got back. He told me his dog was not a criminal or baggage, and ordered me to come back and get its car, at which point the phone went dead.

I returned to the garage with the van, but without the dog, to find the same chauffeur waiting for me. He was full of apologies as he handed me the keys for the dog's car, in which I returned to the house.

Once again, I called the dog. Again he rose and walked out to the car, but this time he jumped in through the open passenger's door and lay down on the back seat with a big satisfied grin on his face. Heaven knows what the family thought about a dog that had a Bentley convertible!

HO3 L
DOG 1

Skinny Dipping

Bongo was not the only hotel canine, although he was the boss dog and quite a character. There was another younger and smaller Labrador and a totally mad boxer.

The hotel had a beautiful open-air swimming pool, set in a fenced-off area situated just under the owner's flat.

One hot summer's evening as it was approaching midnight, Mr C, the hotel owner, came bustling into the office with his walking stick in hand. "Where are the dogs?" he shouted, "Quick, villagers in the pool!" He mustered me with the dogs and we walked briskly out in the dark to the pool.

On arrival, he unlocked the gates and let the dogs in to run around the pool. The dogs were barking at the swimmers in the moonlit pool, who were now all huddled in the middle of the deep end, while shouting at us to call the dogs off, for although they barked a lot, they were certainly not guard dogs.

Mr C casually walked round the pool picking up the bundles of clothes, handing them to me or throwing them into the pool. It appeared most of the male outer clothes came my way, while the rest along with the female clothing went into the pool.

We then had a brisk walk with the dogs back to the hotel, leaving the pool gate open. We never received a complaint from any of our late night swimmers, or a request to lost property for clothes. The odd bits of money we found went to charity. "It paid for their swim, albeit an expensive one!" said Mr C with a big smile.

Wrong Manager

In the summer, on finishing a day or morning shift, I often went for a swim in the hotel open-air pool. In fact, I kept a pair of swimming trunks in the office along with my golf clubs.

On this particular day, it was exceptionally warm so on completing our morning shift, two managers and I, still dressed in our formal morning suits, went straight from work to the pool for a swim. On arrival, we each picked a changing hut, got into our swimming gear, hung up our work suits and went into the pool for a relaxing half hour.

Refreshed after my swim, I returned to the changing hut to dress, put my underpants on, then my shirt, but there was something wrong with my new pinstriped trousers. I realised someone had cut both legs off from the knees, and they'd cut my jacket sleeves off too.

Fuming, I walked back to my office in my new tailored pinstriped shorts, and sleeveless jacket, to the laughter of staff and managers alike. I was determined to find out who did it and why. On questioning the front office and ground staff, I got my answer. The culprit had been seen leaving the pool area and running down the hotel drive with his suitcase, but why had he cut up my suit was still a mystery to me.

Johnny, the food and beverage manager, who I had been swimming with, had the answer: he had sacked the culprit that morning. Johnny had given the culprit, a kitchen porter, two hours to leave the hotel. It seems just enough time for him to get his revenge but, unfortunately for me, he cut up the wrong manager's suit! It took me weeks to get the money out of the hotel for a new suit but I did manage to procure a better and more expensive one.

The Very Shy Bridegroom

In this luxury hotel, we had both twin-bedded and double-bedded suites, each with large bathrooms and sitting areas with superb views. The double-bedded suites were marketed and normally sold as honeymoon suites. The fewer twin-bedded suites could take an extra bed or cot, and were normally sold as luxury family rooms, or on occasions, we removed all the beds and used them as conference syndicate rooms.

I remember this particular Saturday with great embarrassment and regret. The hotel was absolutely full. We had eleven honeymoon couples staying but only ten doubled-bedded honeymoon suites. To accommodate the extra couple, we converted one of the twins to a double-bedded suite.

A simple task: take the twin beds and join them together. The inner bed legs are clamped together and a thin seven-foot mattress is placed vertically over the top, to give a very large comfortable double bed.

It was just after 10pm and all the guests had arrived, when the bell on the desk of the outer reception area rang. I went out from the inner office to the counter to see a young gentleman standing about a yard back from the open counter, looking up and down the corridor.

I asked if I could help him, to which he came right over to me and almost whispered, "I'm in the honeymoon suite on the first floor. It's a bit embarrassing. My wife sat on the bed and it came apart. We did nothing, she really is quite upset about it."

I told him, "Don't worry, I will personally go and fix it." I asked him to collect his wife, take her down to the bar and have a drink on me, while I went up and fixed the bed. I explained, "It's merely a catch on the bed not being connected properly."

I asked him to give me five minutes to get there and another fifteen minutes to fix it. He thanked me, turned and started to walk away. I opened the door behind me and stepped back into the inner office, where the rest of the reception team were sitting having a coffee.

I had only taken a couple of paces when one of the guys asked what the problem was. I said, "Oh, a couple in the honeymoon suite with the cross mattresses must have been giving it a real hammering and it's come apart." From behind me, a high pitched, somewhat distressed voice said, "No we haven't." I spun round as the man turned and ran from the office. No one laughed.

After ten minutes, I phoned the room to check it was empty before going up and fixing the bed, leaving a large bouquet of flowers and an apology note on the bed.

To save any further embarrassment, I went in late the following day, after checking they'd left the hotel.

Meeting the Traffic Cops

Some years ago, I worked in Yorkshire for a family company with two large and very popular restaurants, as well as an extensive and successful outside catering enterprise, for which they had a range of vehicles and trailers to transport people and provisions for events. At the time, I was the food and beverage manager in the main restaurant, where I lived along with other company managers and staff. Part of my job included helping at the larger outside catering events.

It was a dark autumn evening and Carl, one of the outside catering chefs, was towing one of the food trailers behind his Land Rover back to base after a busy day catering at the races. Nearing Ripon, he heard an emergency vehicle siren approaching from behind. He pulled into the side of the road as a police car raced past him and signalled him to stop. Two hundred yards later, Carl was able to pull safely into a lay-by behind the police car. The two police officers exited their car and started to walk towards him.

One policeman went over to the passenger side, while the other walked to the driver's side and stood beside Carl, who lowered the window and asked what the problem was. The police officer, with a smile on his face, asked if the day had been good for business. Carl replied, "Yes, not bad." The policeman then said, "I see you didn't sell all the chickens or the apple pies." A look of amazement came over Carl's face when he asked, "How do you know that?"

The policeman replied, “Well, about a mile back, as we came up behind you, we were hit by four chickens that, although cooked, flew out of the back of your trailer, closely followed by a couple of apple pies still in large baking trays! Now, although we didn’t get to eat them, they’ve caused considerable damage to our police car. If you would like to step out, we’ll show you.”

Carl followed the policeman over to the front of their car, which had a few large dents on the bonnet and several pieces of apple pie stuck to the windscreen. They returned to the back of the trailer, where the roller door was half open.

Carl apologised profusely and assured them he’d padlocked the trailer before setting off. On closer inspection, the police noticed he had put the padlock on, but only through the ring on the door and not the ring on the trailer, allowing the pull-down door to bounce open.

He didn’t get away with it. As the two policemen sat in the police car eating apple pie, his ticket for having an unsafe load was written!

He was fined and the company paid for the repair of the police car. From that day on, Carl always insisted on having two padlocks on trailer doors and he still believes he locked the trailer door properly.

POLICE

The Lost Trailer

Michael had a somewhat different problem when he arrived back at base late one night from a racecourse. He parked the Land Rover at the back of the warehouse and went with John, the warehouse lad, to unhook the trailer and push it into the garage, when to his surprise it wasn't there!

Michael had been working extremely hard since five o'clock in the morning, and it was now just after midnight. He knew he was going to have to drive twenty miles back to the racecourse and pick up the trailer he had stupidly forgotten to hook onto the back of the Land Rover. Many expletives poured forth from his mouth as he begged for one of the staff to go with him but no one offered.

About an hour later, just as I was getting into bed, the phone in the corridor outside my room rang. I didn't think anyone else was around to answer it so I got up. I opened my room door, to meet Pete, one of the chefs, just picking it up, and as I turned to go back to bed, he shouted, "Hold on, Brian! Michael's just back from the racecourse and the trailer's missing. What should he do?" "Call the police," I said. Turning back to my room, I fell into my bed, exhausted after a long day.

In the morning, just after nine o'clock, the police arrived seeking further information about the missing trailer. I left them in the office with Michael and went into the kitchen to have a chat with the chef about the day's business. On entering,

I glanced out the window and there was the missing trailer parked up against the kitchen window! "He's forgotten where he parked it," I said to a somewhat bemused chef.

I went back to the office and interrupted the police interview, saying I needed to have a quick word with Michael. I took him to the kitchen window to show him the trailer and asked, "Is this the trailer you're looking for?" He stood and stared at it, "I never left it there, boss. I went straight round to the garage, honest I did."

We went out to give it a quick check and, yes, it was still locked, although covered in scratches and mud, like it had been through a field. We decided to go back to the office and explain to the waiting police what we thought may have happened. I explained, "It appears one of our staff saw Michael leave the racecourse without the trailer, and towed it back to base, before going home." Everybody was happy, including the police, who left with our sincere apologies.

Later, on opening the trailer, all the equipment and food trays were still inside, but to our surprise, the food was gone.

On investigation, we found that no member of staff had brought the trailer back. It was a mystery for nearly a year before we learned what actually happened. A farmer at a race meeting was overheard by one of our managers, telling one of his friends of his good fortune some months earlier in finding on his land a trailer (our trailer) packed with salmon, chickens and lovely desserts!

From this, we deduced Michael had left the racecourse with the trailer, but it must have been only partially secured to the Land Rover. On an S-bend near to the race course, the trailer and car parted, with the trailer ending up in the farmer's field.

The farmer, being a reasonably honest Yorkshire man, had returned the trailer and, not wishing to create a fuss or send a bill for his time and effort, had emptied it of the perishable food. Evidently, the evening after the event, his friends and family had enjoyed an excellent gourmet dinner, and no action other than laughter was ever taken. Although we never did understand how it became unlocked and then relocked.

Look for the Easy Way

There's always another way of doing things, but sometimes when we're stressed, we only see one way when in fact, there's sometimes a simpler way. This story happened one busy evening, when I was managing the main restaurant.

A number of staff lived in a couple of flats above the restaurant. Three guys lived in the small flat on the first floor next to the private dining and meeting rooms, and the female staff, of which there were about twelve, lived in the three large flats on the floor above.

My assistant Peter and I had just finished closing the restaurant. I suggested he did the cashing up while I went up to the flat to make us some coffee, to which he agreed. About half an hour later, I thought it strange there was still no sign of Peter. I remember thinking he should have cashed up by now. I waited a few more minutes before going to search for him, now a little concerned for his safety.

On my way back to the office, I checked the locks of all the external and security doors, just in case we had intruders. Arriving at the office, I could see Peter lying on the floor with the desks and chairs all over the place. I rushed in, thinking we had been robbed and asked if he was okay.

Peter, who was a rather large lad, looked up at me and laughed. I was still shocked at seeing him on the floor and the office in such a mess. "What happened here?" I asked, "What's taken you so long? Did you fall over and hurt yourself?" Still laughing, he explained.

“I bent down and put the money in the safe, but must have caught my tie in the door when I shut it. With my tie in the safe door, it wouldn’t open. It was jammed shut. I was trapped by my tie. I could only move a little before the tie started to choke me.

Looking round, I saw a pair of scissors on the desk and thought if I cut the tie, it would release me from the safe. So still with my tie caught in the safe, I managed to move a chair with my feet and catch the leg of the desk, but the chair tipped.

Luckily, the chair base was still caught behind the table leg, and I was able to pull the chair and table over with my foot.

Then, using both feet, I managed to shake the table enough for the tray to fall off, throwing the scissors onto the floor. Finally, with my feet, I managed to manoeuvre the scissors up to my hand and cut the tie, thankfully releasing me from the safe, just as you arrived.”

I looked at him lying there, totally exhausted by his series of complex exertions to get to the scissors and release his tie from the safe and asked, “Why didn’t you just undo the tie and take it off over your head?” to which he replied, “It never occurred to me. I just saw the scissors and thought I needed to cut the tie to release me from the safe!”

I have to say it was quite expensive for the locksmith to open the safe and get Peter back the remainder of his tie.

The Oyster Bar

The restaurant had a very busy and fashionable oyster bar, used by the elite of both Harrogate and Leeds. The bar itself was situated several yards from the main kitchen and communication was via an intercom system.

Since joining the restaurant three months earlier as Food and Beverage Manager, I had never worked in the bar. Most of my work during the service of meals was in the kitchen, checking the food before it went out to the customers, in the restaurants and the oyster bar.

My embarrassing experience was due to a combination of sudden staff illness and holidays, resulting in the oyster bar being understaffed on what was going to be a very busy lunchtime, including a party of twenty booked from the BBC in Leeds.

I decided I would need to go to the oyster bar and help the staff. Up to this time, my role in the oyster bar service had been at the kitchen-end of the intercom system, where I would listen for the call from the bar, note the order on paper and pass it to the kitchen. When the food was ready, I would press my 'on' button, buzz the bar and say table 'whatever' was ready for collection.

On my arrival to start work in the bar, it was already full and my first task was to take a somewhat complex order from the BBC party of twenty.

Having taken the order, I quickly walked back behind the bar counter to the intercom. I pressed the buzzer and proceeded to read out the order in my normal speaking voice, "Four soup, two consommé, three times six oysters, two smoked salmon starters, three mussels, four regular paté, two buttered shrimps, and could you provide additional warm rolls and six rounds of thick brown bread toast."

On finishing reading out the order, I quickly picked up a jug of iced water and walked back to the table. I was in the middle of pouring the first glass when, loud and clear over the intercom, a somewhat annoyed sous chef shouted, "What the bloody hell do you think I am, a chef or a shorthand typist? I can't write at that speed. Repeat the bloody order slowly!"

In panic, forgetting I still had the jug of water in my hand, I started to run back behind the bar to the intercom terminal, to turn it off. In my haste, I spilled a little water over the floor, slipped on it and went crashing into the bar counter, thankfully still in an upright position but the damage to my credibility was done.

The BBC group, who I presume were perfectly used to communication cock-ups, were in fits of laughter as I stumbled back behind the bar, turned the machine off and ran on to the kitchen where I handed the chef the paper order.

On my return to the bar, I went round the tables apologising for the mishap with the intercom but thankfully everyone except me had found it amusing.

Fortunately, they all enjoyed their meal and the BBC party thought it was one of the funniest lunchtimes they ever had. I certainly didn't!

After the service, the chef was very apologetic. He assumed I'd turned the volume down after giving the order, but not being proficient in the use of the intercom in the bar, instead I'd turned it right up. Still, we did see the funny side of it.

I couldn't even get old technology right, so what chance do I have today?

Car Parking

Another case of trainee driving disasters came some time later. I had an old Morris Minor Traveller, and I became competent at doing handbrake turns in the restaurant's large gravel car park. I got very good at it and after a few months, I could park the car rather neatly into one of the larger than average car parking spaces, each pair of which was separated by a four foot high beech hedge.

Young Percy, a man of good Yorkshire farming stock, joined the staff as a trainee manager and, after a couple of weeks watching me show off my handbrake turns and parking skills, decided it was time for him to have a go.

Not being a complete idiot, Percy was waiting for a day when the car park was empty before trying his handbrake turns. It was a Sunday morning, I remember it well. The owner had arrived unusually early. He popped into my office, wished me a good morning and told me he was in early to sort the banking from the previous day's outside catering, before going on a family day out. A little later, I was sitting in the front bar area having breakfast, looking out over the car park.

I watched Percy arrive in his Land Rover, drive a little fast across the car park and, near the far end, he turned sideways, did a 360 degree spin, and carried on straight through one of the dividing beech hedges, crashing into a car parked and hidden behind the hedge!

Hearing the crash, I jumped up and rushed out to make sure

he was okay and find out what happened. I arrived to find him sitting in his Land Rover looking a bit dazed. I asked, "What happened?" He explained he'd been trying to do a handbrake turn, had pulled on the handbrake and turned the wheel, like he had seen me do on many occasions, but then everything went wrong. There was an almighty crash from under the car and the Land Rover went totally out of his control. The brake was just not working.

To make matters worse, he hadn't noticed the car behind the hedge and unfortunately, hit it right in the middle, totally destroying it.

I looked at the car he'd just wiped out and cringed. I immediately recognised it: the owner's brand new Austin Princess, no more than one month old, his pride and joy and the car he was going to be taking the family out in later that day. As I turned back to help Percy out of the Land Rover, I saw Mr Brook, the owner, walking briskly towards us.

I won't write what I called Percy, or what Mr Brook said to him before he turned and stormed off back to the restaurant, leaving Percy and I to sort out the mess. After that, Percy and I returned to the office, he to phone his Dad while I went to console Mr Brook and try to lower his temper.

A few minutes later, Percy's father arrived and asked to see Mr Brook. I took him through and left him and Mr Brook alone in the office. It was about half an hour later they emerged and shook hands. A few minutes later, Percy was called to the office and on leaving, he smiled and gave me the thumbs up.

Percy had kept his job and his wealthy father had agreed to pay for a new car and for the hire of a vehicle until it arrived. The only real setback was the banning of handbrake parking in the car park.

After the incident, we found out that the handbrake on a Land Rover is not connected to the wheels like on a normal car but to the drive shaft, and what Percy did had broken the drive shaft, leaving the car totally uncontrollable.

The Coach Party Booking Room

I spent much of my life working with coach parties in the summer, they could account for up to 70% of our hotel accommodation. My introduction to working with coach tours started in the head office of a major UK hotel company, and, yes, it was before we had computers to record bookings.

In the late 60s and 70s, for tours and bookings over ten rooms, we used pin boards. This enabled us to identify the capacity of 4,600 bedrooms in our thirty-plus hotels throughout the country. The boards covered the four walls of the central booking office, providing at a glance the availability in every one of the company hotels – fantastic.

It worked really well until one evening a clumsy cleaner fell against the wall and knocked half the pins off. Realising what she'd done, she picked the pins up from the floor and put them back in the boards, but not where they came out. A couple of days after her fall, we received a confirmation of a large booking and when I went to check and change the pins on the chart, I noticed something was wrong. It took two of us three days to find out which hotel's pins had been changed and to check every booking in the affected twelve hotels for the next two years.

Once we realised so many pins had been moved, an investigation was undertaken to discover how or who was responsible. The cleaner quickly owned up and once she realised the impact of her error was really upset. She brought us a tin of biscuits and promised to be much more careful in the future.

I have to say computers are far more accurate but the pin boarded walls were quicker at enabling us to identify at a glance where there were vacancies still to be filled.

International Miscommunications

A long time ago, before the worldwide-web and email existed, communication was via telegram, telephone, telex and tele-printer. At this time, I was working as a sales assistant in the group and tour bookings office of a large hotel company's head office in London. This tale began soon after I started in September and includes Bernard, a senior member of our sales team, who at the time was in South America on a sales drive

A telex arrived for me from Bernard. It read, "Brian, have provisional booking for two charters, 1,100 in each, arrive London Wednesday 6th February, six nights in London then tour Europe, return London 12th March five nights, please confirm availability for booking."

I read it and thought, *Silly fool, planes aren't big enough to hold 1100 people*, so I confirmed back:

'Bernard, confirm booking for two charters, 110 in each, arrive London Wednesday 6th February, six nights in London then tour Europe, return London 12th March for five nights. Due to timing clashing with the Scotland v England football match on the first weekend, will have to spread them over a number of London hotels.'

Bernard's telex came in a couple of days later, "OK, confirmed."

Once confirmed and the rooms booked between two of our hotels, I forgot all about the booking until early January when the telex went mad. It started to print out the names of the people coming from São Paulo, all 2,200 of them! I rushed into Bernard's office for an explanation, to discover we had each thought the other had made an error in our telex. It was ships not planes and, yes, there were nearly 2,200 people coming… but where on earth was I going to put them all?!

Panic-stricken I phoned Rino, the reception manager at our largest London hotel, where I had booked most of the 220 people. First I asked if he was sitting down, before asking how room bookings were on the football weekend of 8th and 9th February. He replied, "Not too bad, about forty-five rooms overbooked, it should be okay, not all those booked will turn up." I took a deep breath and explained the problem: I was looking for another 950 rooms! Sufficient to say, he was not a happy Spaniard, and rudely informed me, "No way can this hotel or any of our London hotels accommodate another 1,900 people."

Decision time… should I disappear, resign or wait to be sacked? I decided there was no point spending time worrying, it would just make me even more stressed, so apprehensively, I went into the sales director's office to explain the situation and find out when I would be leaving the company.

Well, what a surprise, he was calm, gave me a real dressing down for being sloppy and told me to go back to work. In the afternoon, he called a meeting in the boardroom for all the sales executives and hotel operation directors. We spent the next hour discussing various options until finally the sales director came up with a plan.

Within two days of the meeting, a brochure was produced in Portuguese and English offering a 'Welcome to Europe Weekend Spectacular' for our South American friends; the festive weekend consisting of two nights on 8th and 9th February in any of our UK or European hotels. Travel would be at cost price, for which we had negotiated greatly reduced rates for rail, air and coach travel, and of course, they'd already paid for their accommodation so travel was the only additional cost.

The sales staff met with the tourists as they berthed at Tilbury and travelled in the coaches with them to London, during which they sold the package to over 2,000 of them.

The thing I remember most was the thirty-plus coaches encircling Portland Square, and all our Portuguese-speaking staff directing guests onto their coaches for their European weekend.

I recall it was £6 for the weekend in our four-star hotel in Edinburgh and £10 for our five-star hotel in Paris. For the 150 tourists who decided to stay in London, we managed to open a couple of floors in one of our hotels, which had been closed for redecoration, and gave them a cabaret banquet evening.

The result was a total success with every London, UK and European hotel in the company fully booked, as well as most of the company's UK associate hotels. It was the busiest weekend ever in the history of the company.

How did we do it? Teamwork, and looking at the problem as an opportunity.

What did I learn? Always confirm details, never make assumptions and when you get it wrong, own up and seek help as soon as possible.

Every cloud has a silver lining, although sometimes it's not apparent at the time, and, of course, I was very lucky working for a fantastic team of truly inspirational professionals.

Why No Breakfast?

The Development of Tourism Act 1969, with its incentive grants, brought a flurry of new hotels in London and throughout the UK. Hotel companies expanded at a spectacular rate, with new hotels and extensions to existing ones. The company I worked for had a wide range of hotels, from small three star ones to large, luxury five-star hotels.

In the late 1960s and early 70s, Stardbank Holidays brought about enormous changes in London hotels. It opened them to thousands of people who'd never stayed in a large hotel. Stardbank sold weekend breaks at cost plus a little towards profit, enabling our hotels to be full nearly every night of the week. Until then, most London Hotels were busy with business guests Monday to Thursday and almost empty at the weekends.

I particularly remember dealing with a couple of complaints when working in the sales office. People would travel on chartered trains from all over the UK to stay in our London hotels and, of course, many had never stayed in a hotel before. One complaint was from a very well-spoken lady living in Tunbridge Wells. She and her friend had been staying in one of our more exclusive London hotels. The conversation went like this:

"The reception staff gave us a wonderful welcome and Saturday night's dinner was excellent: superb food and the waiting staff were just so attentive. However, we were so disappointed at not getting our breakfast on the Sunday morning. We waited in our room till 11.30am when, as you will know, we had to check out. We just had to leave without our breakfast. It was such a disappointing end to what had been a wonderful weekend in London."

Knowing many of our hotels were often very busy at breakfast, I explained I would look into it and get back to her. I checked with the hotel and discovered there were no delays for breakfast on the Sunday morning. In fact, everyone was served quickly and there were no complaints.

Now somewhat puzzled, I phoned the lady in Tunbridge Wells and asked what time she'd gone down to the restaurant for breakfast. "Oh, we didn't go down to the restaurant. The reception staff told us we could have breakfast in our bedroom from room service at no extra cost. We thought that would be really lovely and make an excellent finish to our stay, but our breakfast never came."

I asked what time she'd ordered breakfast. There was a pregnant pause and then she said, "We didn't think you had to order it. We thought it just came automatically."

I smiled to myself as I explained sympathetically how room service operated. She hastily apologised for making such a fuss about something which was obviously their fault.

I tried to put her at ease and, during the conversation, she told me this had been their first stay in a luxury London hotel and they were so sorry for causing so much trouble.

I tactfully explained it was not a problem and as gesture of goodwill gave them a free night's bed and breakfast in the same hotel. This time I received no more complaints, just a note of thanks. I guess they ordered breakfast at their next visit!

Room Sharing

I received this complaint from a gentleman calling from Newcastle, which is best read in a Geordie accent. Sorry, if my attempt to write it phonetically doesn't do his accent justice.

"Ah just thowt Ah should phone an' say if ye want folk te share a bed wi' a stranger, ye should tell them when ye givin' them the room."

I assured the caller we did not expect guests to share and would he tell me a bit more so I could investigate and get back to him.

"Weel," he said, "Ah come doon on the train with the rest o' the lads from the factory and it was great. Nivver bin on a lang train journey afore. Anyway, Ah gets te London and gans wi' the lads on the Tube to the Bostyn 'otel. It was grand. The manager met me and the lads at reception, an' explained that there'd bin a bit of a problem wi' the rooms. Ye see, the decorators 'adn't finished the job but they'd booked us inte one of the company's posher 'otels. He teks us oot and paiys for a taxi to tek the four of us there. When the taxi got te the next 'otel, this bloke in a top hat come oot an' carried wor bags to the grandest hall Ah've ivver bin in. That Europe 'otel! Ah'm not kiddin', the carpet was that thick, ye had te craal through it. Anyway, Ah gets inte the room, bloody hell, Ah thowt, it was bigger than wor hoose, wi' a massive bed in the middle. Weel, Ah met up wi' the lads and went te the early matinee show. Man, that was custy too, nivver seen a London show, then a couple o' pints and summat te eat then back te the 'otel for an early neet.

Weel, aboot two in the mornin', the door oppens an' this bloke comes inte me room. Ah could tell 'e was a bit tiddly, 'e stunk o' booze an' 'e kept fallin' doon tryin' te tek 'is claes off. Anyway, 'e gets in the bed an' gans te sleep. Ah tried te ask 'im if 'e was in the reet room but Ah think 'e was foreign 'cos Ah couldn't understan' a word 'e was sayin'. Anyway, when Ah wakes up at six, 'e was gone, an' Ah nivver seen his bags, like."

Somewhat amazed, I said to the man from Newcastle that I would look into it and get back to him. These are my findings:

The gentleman from Newcastle had been booked into the Bostyn, a three-star hotel which was overbooked, so he was transferred to the company's five-star Europe hotel.

The gentleman who arrived in his room in the middle of the night was a Frenchman, who'd also been booked out of one of our other overbooked hotels and transferred to the unfinished, brand new five-star Brit Hotel on the other side of the square to the Europe.

Unfortunately, he'd been given the same room number in the Brit Hotel as the man in the Europe, and even more strange, it appears the large plastic key fob he was given was a Europe one, as the Brit ones for the floor he was staying on hadn't arrived. But when it had been given to him, the Europe name had been taped over and a Brit hotel sticker put on it.

The next part is assumption: the sticker must have come off the key fob and the man, being very drunk and with little grasp of English, had gone to the Europe Hotel in accordance with the label on his key fob.

The next part is fact: he'd gone to the room indicated on the key fob and not been able to get in with his key, as it was the right room number but the wrong hotel. He went down to reception for help to get into his room. He indicated in sign language to the night porter that his key wouldn't open his door. The night porter, seeing it was the right room number on the key fob, went up and he too couldn't get the door to open, but, using his master key, opened the door and the Frenchman went in.

I phoned the man in Newcastle to apologise for our series of errors and explained what had happened, but he just kept laughing and saying, "Eee, Ah'll get a few pints off the lads when Ah tell them this." I bet he did, even if only from the refund we sent him.

Keeping the After Eights Safe

Some years ago, I was employed in Scotland at a medium-sized hotel by the sea. The hotel had four main markets: golfers, business conferences, banqueting and families in the summer holidays. It was there I employed Colin as the banqueting manager. He was young, enthusiastic and came with exemplary references, including superb sales and customer skills, along with a reputation for being exceptionally efficient. In fact, he was just what we needed at the time.

At the end of his first week, we met to discuss a number of topics and he produced a rather long list of things he felt could be improved. We discussed how he wished to implement the improvements and it was as we were finishing the meeting that he casually mentioned the 'After Eights', which were served with the coffee at all banquets. His concern was the number of sweets disappearing between being laid out for the service and actually being served to the customers.

He presumed staff were eating them because at the last function, before the service he personally made up a plate for each table with the correct number of After Eights, but the guests on several tables had complained there were insufficient mints.

He was convinced staff were stealing them but, not to worry, he had a plan: at the next dinner none would be stolen and every guest would get their After Eight.

I was checking the room just before the next night's banquet was about to start and failed to see any After Eights set out on the service tables. I asked Colin, "What, no After Eights tonight, Colin?" "No," he replied, "I have it sorted. The staff won't be eating them tonight. They're all plated up in the safe." "Bit overkill," I said. "Probably," he replied, "but tonight we'll have enough to go round and possibly a few over."

An hour and a half later, as the coffee was being served, I bumped into Colin as he was rushing down to the food store. A few minutes later, he passed me with several boxes of After Eights on his way to the banquet.

The next day, Colin explained. He'd staked the After Eights on plates in the safe. Unfortunately, the weight of the plates had crushed all but the top tiers of After Eights and those underneath were totally squashed and ruined.

He had wasted over 120 After Eights, far more than staff ever nicked. The next week, the After Eight plates were all out in the banqueting service area but covered with Clingfilm, a far better, safer and more effective solution than the safe.

So remember, the safe is not always the safest place.

The Zealous Kitchen Porter

Good, reliable kitchen porters are key to the efficient running of any commercial kitchen. They range from young students looking for a bit of extra cash, ex-prisoners who find that hotels offering accommodation are a huge asset in their rehabilitation, and sometimes those with learning difficulties who find the friendly, supportive atmosphere of a hotel the ideal working environment.

This incident occurred on a Saturday night just before ten o'clock. The dinner in the function room had been served and the last customers had left the restaurant. The chef and I were sitting in his office, deep in conversation, analysing the day's business.

We looked up and there in the doorway was Roger, the kitchen porter, who, with his usual big smile, lifted his hand up from his chest and gave us a little wave. We both acknowledged his wave and, thinking Roger was leaving, carried on our conversation, but he just stood there looking at us. After a couple of minutes, the chef said, "Yes Roger, what can we do for you?"

"Well, chef, I'm just going home as I have to catch the ten o'clock bus because if I get home late Mrs Mair, my landlady, gets really upset. You know, one night the bus was cancelled and she was so upset, she called the police, and they picked me up and took me home. She was so worried, she hit me with the *Daily Mail* and told me not to be late again so I thought before I go and get the bus I should just tell you the kitchen's on fire!"

We both leapt up and flew out of the office, grabbing a couple of fire extinguishers and fire blankets on the way. In the kitchen, we found a large pot of oil in flames on the stove. We turned off the gas and smothered the pot with the blanket, putting the fire out, while Roger casually walked out of the kitchen to catch his bus. We were very lucky. A couple of minutes later the kitchen could have been engulfed in flames.

The next day, Roger turned up for work as usual and we thanked him for waiting to tell us about the fire. Later in the month, he and Mrs Mair, his landlady, were invited to the hotel for a special lunch, where Roger was presented with a certificate of thanks from the company, which at his request was hung with pride in the kitchen. Both it and Roger were still there long after I left.

Agency Chefs

There are some excellent agency chefs, but this is the story of one who turned out to be neither chef nor cook.

It was Wednesday and we had a large function coming on the Saturday, plus a full hotel with a residential conference. The head chef asked if I could get him a chef to help out for the weekend, as one of his assistant chefs was in hospital having a minor operation. I called the local employment agency to request a good chef to help us out for at least three days. About an hour later, they phoned back saying they had an experienced chef who was free to come and help.

He arrived on the Friday morning, looking immaculate, and the head chef left him working with the team preparing the vegetables and starters for the day. All appeared to be going well.

The problem started about six o'clock the next evening, when a very agitated head chef called me down to the kitchen.

I arrived at his office and he took me into the cold room preparation area, where I stood with him and watched in amazement. There were 150 small plates with a bed of lettuce on them, each with two half boiled eggs placed neatly in the middle, onto which this so-called chef was carefully pouring custard. He explained that he was told to make 150 individual egg custards.

After the head chef had cooled down, the man explained he had just got it mixed up with egg mayonnaise. A simple mistake anyone could make… anyone who wasn't a cook!

COWBOY
CHEF

Pet Duck in the Basement

On one very rainy mid-morning, the chef and I were walking down the long basement corridor between the main and conference kitchens, when, to our amazement, we spied a lovely young mallard duck walking towards us. Both being regular duck hunters, we walked slowly towards it, trying not to scare it off.

I bent down and grabbed it. Holding it closely to my chest with one hand, I started turning its head round several times with the other hand. I was ready to give it a sharp tug when I heard a very high pitched scream from the far end of the corridor.

"Percy, my Percy, my poor Percy, why, there you are!" I swiftly let go of its head which spun round like a top as I dropped the pet duck back to the floor, where it waddled off quickly, happily and somewhat dizzily back down the corridor to its owner, our new neighbour, who lovingly picked it up.

Pity really, it would have been great with orange sauce!

The Call from the Prison

Kitchen porters, as I have said before, are sometimes people with problems, including having nowhere to live, so they find employment with accommodation a great attraction. This story relates to one of these gentlemen.

Mark had been employed for just over three months. He was an excellent worker, enthusiastic and well liked. However, Mark had a drink problem and he knew if he was paid on a Friday night, he wouldn't sober up till Monday, so, at his request, we paid him on Sunday after lunch, and he was off duty till Tuesday night when he would return bright and sober, but normally broke.

It was a surprise when one Tuesday Mark failed to turn up for work. Concerned for him, the chef and I went down the road to his room in the staff house. We found his room tidy and clean, with his clothes laid out, but no Mark. We walked back to the hotel and, on questioning other staff, discovered he'd gone to Glasgow to meet family and perhaps he'd been held up.

Well, Friday came along and at about 10am, a phone call was put through to me. It was the assistant governor at Barlinnie Prison. They had Mark in custody on an outstanding warrant. He explained that Mark would be in prison for the next four weeks and he'd requested for me to be telephoned to ask if he could possibly have his job back when he was released in four weeks' time. If not, he would understand but, if that was the case, could we pack his belongings and he would collect them when released.

I said we would keep his job and was just about to put the phone down when he said, “Oh yes, I do have another important thing to tell you. Mark has a pet in his room.” I said, “But the chef and I went down there on Tuesday and we saw no pet.” To which the Governor replied, “Well, it’s a pet snake, I assume a grass snake.” I thanked him for the information and marched down to the kitchen to see the chef.

Now Teddy the chef and I were good mates and spent much of our free time in the winter rough shooting on a nearby large estate, and dealing with grass snakes was no big deal. Down to the room we went with a couple of sticks and a large canvas bag for the snake.

I must say there’s something a bit scary about crawling under a bed, poking in a wardrobe and ruffling through clothes in a chest of drawers looking for a hungry snake that could be anywhere. We checked behind the curtains, in the sink, in all the neatly piled bags on the floor and finally started to empty the drawers when plop, it fell out, a lovely 50cm long adder… not a grass snake!

We were both stunned it was an adder and relieved it hadn’t been under the furniture, for if cornered, it may well have bitten us and put us in hospital.

We threw the bag over the snake and safely secured, we took it to a nearby wood and released it. We did laugh about the nervous tension it created in us. Four weeks later, Mark got his job back but on the condition of no more snakes or any other pets in his room.

Luggage on Tour

Hotels welcome and look after their coach party guests exceptionally well and, in general, the operation is remarkably efficient.

Arriving guests are greeted either on their coach or in one of the hotel's private rooms, where their booking requirements are checked and the appropriate rooms allocated. Their luggage is unloaded from the coach into a secure area where porters chalk the appropriate room numbers onto each guest's bags, ensuring the correct luggage is reunited with its owner.

The hotel in this story worked with a number of coach companies prioritising tour companies, which provided back-to-back bookings (when one coach party from the company departs in the morning, it's replaced by the next that afternoon). This ensures the hotel could allocate the same rooms to that company's guests throughout the summer.

This recounts the tale of a coach party on a back-to-back allocation touring Scotland. Rather unusually, the coach party wasn't leaving in the morning after breakfast. It was going on a lunchtime tour of Edinburgh before travelling north to their next destination. As usual, their luggage was collected from their rooms just after 9am and put in the hotel luggage store to be loaded onto their coach when it departed in the afternoon.

It was just after 5pm when the duty receptionist entered the office to tell me there was a problem. Five newly arrived guests had phoned to say the wrong luggage had been delivered to their room. She had asked the head porter to check and, at this point, he arrived, explaining a number of guests on a coach party had the wrong cases. His staff were now collecting all of the party's cases and checking them off with the names on the rooming list before distributing them to their rightful owners.

Ten minutes later, he returned and informed me that none of the cases belonged to the coach party guests. In fact, none of them belonged to any of our hotel guests. I was about to phone the coach party's previous hotel to check if the correct luggage had been loaded on their coach when Judy our receptionist arrived and updated me.

The cases we had actually belonged to a coach party that left the hotel that day. The coach parties were from the same company and the previous day's coach had left about the time the latest arrived. A quick meeting with the porters confirmed that the morning shift, before going off duty, had brought the cases in from the arriving coach and placed them in the reception secure area while the evening shift of porters had helped the driver of the departing coach to load these cases onto his coach. Once the departing coach had left, they'd taken the luggage out of the store. They assumed it belonged to the arriving coach and delivered it to the room numbers already chalked on them.

Now this happened long before mobile phones. There was no way of directly contacting the coach. I phoned their next hotel and explained what had happened and offered to come straight away and exchange the luggage. It was a mad rush to hire a van and drive the sixty miles, exchange luggage and return, but by 7pm all was complete. In the meantime, our coach party guests were given a private bar with a free drink and nibbles while they waited for their luggage and dinner. As I entered the bar to inform them dinner was ready and their cases were now in their rooms, I was astonished. They applauded, and no one complained.

It was only later after dinner in the bar, I found there, to my surprise, my cousin Douglas and his wife. They were part of the coach party and had told the guests it was the coach driver's fault for not checking the cases when he put them on the coach. The hotel management had quickly sorted out the problem and hired a van to go and pick up their luggage. I'm so lucky to have good relatives to help me out of a jam and he never did tell the coach party we were related.

The next morning, we received a number of complimentary remarks on our quick response to the problem. Still, I think our staff got a shock, for from then on we also checked cases onto the coaches and took great care to ensure we got it right.

Guest's Surprise

It was about seven o'clock one evening when reception informed me the toilet flush in room 404 wasn't working. As the hotel maintenance staff had left for the day, I made my way up to the room.

I knocked on the door, entered and explained to the couple that I was the manager and was here to fix the toilet. I went into their bathroom to check the toilet and, sure enough, the handle wasn't working. A common fault: the wire pin in the cistern, which connected to the handle, had broken, resulting in it not working. I explained to the couple I had to fix it in the service area.

Hotels of this period had a service chute between the bathrooms of the en-suite bedrooms.

I took my passkey and opened the narrow service area which housed odd spares, fuse boxes and plumbing, including the toilet flushing tanks. I could see room 404's cistern pin had broken. I quickly replaced the broken part with a spare one and flushed the toilet to check it worked. Then, on turning round to leave, I casually flushed the toilet behind me, that of room 402.

Guess my surprise when I heard through the wall of room 402 a high-pitched woman's voice shout, "Hey, George, this one's automatic!"

I quietly crept out and locked the service door, hoping that next time she wouldn't wait for the automatic flush.

Fair Cop, Gov

At the time of this story, most people didn't have bank accounts, and the majority of staff wages were paid in cash weekly. Also, not all houses had a telephone and mobile phones were still to arrive.

I'd just been promoted to the management of a large London West End hotel and it was payday. The personnel manager phoned to tell me that Frank, the wages clerk, would not be in. His wife had phoned from her work to tell us that he'd eaten something a bit dodgy the night before, and had food poisoning.

A couple of minutes later, the personnel manager phoned again to tell me there was a problem. The wages safe key was not in the main safe. Frank must have it at home and she had no way of contacting him.

I had a choice. I could either collect the key from his flat a couple of minutes from the hotel, or get the spare key held at the company's head office three miles away across London.

I was about to make the decision, when two of our local uniformed police entered my office to report on the finding of some property stolen from the hotel. As they were about to leave, I asked if they could do me a favour and go round to Frank's flat and collect the safe key for me. They both agreed and off they went.

It was an hour before they returned with the safe key, which I promptly dispatched to the hotel personnel manager to check the safe and get the wages paid. I'd been worried in case Frank had absconded with the staff wages.

At this point, the police officers sat down, I assumed for a coffee, so I offered it but unusually they refused. They told me they'd just arrested Frank and were about to go back to the police station, where he was being held on charges of theft. I was rather shocked to say the least, as they proceeded to tell me what had happened.

They knocked on his door and when he opened it Frank stammered out, "How did you find out? I really needed the money. Okay I'll come quietly. I knew someone would find out. I should have left!" Somewhat bewildered, but not stupid, the policemen pretended they knew all about what he was confessing to, and let him carry on telling them about how he'd been robbing the hotel for the last twelve months.

He'd been paying himself the wages for a member of staff who'd left the hotel to go back to Egypt about thirteen months ago. I think he ended up in prison for about the same period of time.

It's strange what effect illness and the police at your door can have on the guilty mind.

Hot Pants

One of the great pleasures of working in a smaller hotel is you get to meet so many interesting and lovely people in more social circumstances than is normally possible in larger hotels.

I was working as an assistant manager in a small eighty-bedroom hotel in the West End of London. Weekday shifts started at 10am and finished at 3pm the next day. At weekends, they started at 6pm on Friday evening through to 11am on the Monday. I should say we did get to sleep at night, although this was often disturbed.

With the hotel having a limited number of staff, my duties included working in the bar and reception area when staff had their breaks and meals. This particular hotel had regular groups of young trainee hairdressers staying while they attended four-week training courses at a nearby hairdressing school. I often met and chatted with them when covering evening breaks for the bar staff.

I remember one particular group's last evening: it was a Friday and they were having an end of course parting celebration, as all but two of them were leaving early the following morning. The remaining two were leaving later on the Saturday evening and, as the hotel was not going to be full, I offered them a complimentary room in which to store their luggage and change clothes during the day.

Like most young hairdressers, they were extremely fashion conscious and the two young ladies staying over on the Saturday were going shopping in Carnaby Street. At the time, Carnaby Street was the most fashionable place for young people in the UK.

The conversation around the bar on the Friday evening was on fashion trends and what they were going to buy at Carnaby Street for themselves and their friends back home. During the evening, Jill, one of the two leaving on the Saturday evening, casually asked what they could get for me as a thank you for providing them with a courtesy room and making their stay enjoyable. In jest I said, "A pair of yellow socks."

After lunch the next day, I was sitting in my office checking the reception arrivals for the day, when, to my surprise, the glass office door opened and in walked Jill. She was dressed in very short yellow hot pants, long boots and a bright red t-shirt that looked more like a belt on this busty young lady.

She strutted across the office and perched her bottom on the edge of my desk, leaned across the desk towards me and threw across a pair of yellow socks, saying, "These are for you, my dear." I was about to reply when the door opened and our company chairman put his head in, but on seeing the situation he left promptly without a word.

I was very embarrassed and had to explain to Jill who he was, after which she laughed and left the office, blowing me a kiss on her way out. Two minutes later, the chairman returned, but this time he locked the door behind him and sat down opposite me with a stern expression on his face. I sat there waiting while he composed himself.

"I suppose she is one of your women," he said. "No, sir," I replied, "more like one of yours. She's been a guest in the hotel for the last three weeks," to which he got up, unlocked the door and left.

I guessed that was not the end of the matter and expected him to go for a walk round the hotel, then come back to deal with me in more detail, and I was right. Ten minutes later he returned, once again locking the door behind him. He stood there, apologised for reading the situation wrongly but gave me a telling-off for not having the door locked!

Later that week, I got a card from Jill telling me that she had waited outside my office for him, where both she and her friend explained to him how much they'd enjoyed their stay in the hotel, how good the management and staff had been… and that the yellow socks were simply a thank you gift!

Poisoned from the Mini Bar

I was seconded for a month to manage the reception area of a large, newly opened London hotel. The hotel was experiencing a number of teething problems, partly due to the inexperience of the recently appointed staff and the new reception manager leaving in his second week.

It was about nine o'clock in the evening when an extremely agitated and large gentleman, dressed only in a towel, rushed up to reception shouting, "Effing hotel, bloody rubbish! I want the manager now or else the police. You shouldn't be poisoned in a hotel!"

I immediately came out of the back office and asked the gentleman to come through to my office rather than stand in reception in only a towel, which had a good chance of falling down with his gestural ranting.

As we entered, he shouted at me, "I go to the bathroom, I run a bath and get in. I like a nice scotch in my bath. I take a swig from the bottle out of the mini bar and it's bloody piss. Here, you taste!" He thrust the small, half empty bottle into my hand.

"No thanks," I replied quite adamantly. There was no way I was going to taste that amber liquid, which I could smell was urine. After a few minutes, he calmed down, especially when I presented him with a fine, large bottle of whisky to take back to his bath.

An hour later he came back and apologised for his language

in front of the ladies, and offered me a swig from his new bottle. I declined, well, you never know! You see, the bottle had been opened!

Telephone Exchange

Technology has definitely moved on. No longer do hotels have manual, tabular ledgers for guest accounting or even use machines like the Sweda '76 cash register. Today, when a customer has a meal or a drink, it's automatically recorded by computer on their bill. Telephone systems too have changed, no more large boards with cords you plug in. They're now so small and automated, enabling you to dial internal and external calls from your bedroom, with no more need for a hotel switchboard.

An example of a hotel switchboard

When I started, we had either a part- or full-time telephonist working on a manual telephone system. The telephone system itself was similar to the one illustrated, with plug-in cords. The public address worked from a built-in microphone sitting at head height, with a lever on the desk to turn it on. One evening, I remember a night porter came into the reception area, sat on the edge of the telephone exchange, and proceeded to tell his colleagues about a sexual experience he'd had earlier that evening with a young lady.

His story brought managers and staff running to reception from all areas of the hotel. He'd been sitting on the public address lever and his conversation was being heard in the hotel's five bars, three restaurants and main function suite! Fortunately, it was 11pm and most of the guests had gone to bed. In my experience, not even during a fire drill have I seen managers and staff move so quickly.

Is that reception?

On another occasion, I remember a guest who continually phoned down to reception for the most trivial things, to either complain or compliment the reception staff. Once on the phone, he was difficult to get off.

It appeared he just wanted to chat with someone. The reception staff got so fed up with him continually taking up their time that one receptionist, Pam, put him through to her grandmother who lived locally, and left him chatting to her for over an hour. Pam's surprise came a fortnight later during the gentleman's next stay, when her grandmother turned up to have dinner with him. I never approved of receptionists as dating agencies, but I hope they got on well.

Umbrellas Provided

Like all of the large older London hotels in the 1970s, maintenance was a continual task, involving in-house maintenance departments as well as the daily flow of external contractors. It wasn't unusual for the duty manager to be called to deal with a problem in the early hours of the morning when the maintenance staff were at home.

This was one of those nights. There was a summer gale blowing and I'd retired to my room just after midnight. I was dozing off when the phone rang. The head night porter explained there was a problem with water leaking into a room. When he asked if I would come and help, I dressed and went down to reception to find a somewhat irate gentleman in his dressing gown complaining bitterly about his room.

It appeared that a very small part of the ceiling had come down, followed by about half a mug of water, landing on the floor at the foot of his bed. I pacified him a little by pointing out his good luck that it had not landed on the bed! I arranged another room for him, cancelled his room bill and went with him to help move his belongings, while continuing to apologise and calm him down.

With the irate guest pacified, I returned to reception to quiz the night staff about the leak. They explained that they'd phoned the room above and been told everything was okay. I asked if they'd actually been in the room above, to which they said no. So off I went with the head night porter to check the vacated room, which now had a bucket to catch the occasional drips. Then we went upstairs, as I got the feeling the room the porter had phoned was not directly over where the ceiling had come down.

I explained to the night porter that my doubt may have been due to the quirkiness of the conversion in the building. To check, we measured the distance from the lift on both floors and discovered there were in fact two rooms directly above, and it appeared more probable it wasn't the room phoned but the other room. We could hear the television and see a light shining in the room from under the door, so I knocked on the door and a voice with an Eastern accent shouted back, "Come."

Imagine my astonishment on entering the room to find a young Japanese couple sitting on the bed under a large umbrella, with the rain cascading in from an open skylight. I stepped onto the bed beside them and shut the skylight, to their applause and a rousing, "Thankee, thankee!"

I asked why they left the window open but they didn't appear to understand. Having no more spare rooms, we changed the bed linen, dried the floor and left them sitting on the bed, watching television and giggling away.

Introducing Colour Televisions

On a number of occasions, I worked in hotel company head offices, in both sales and audit departments. These were indeed beneficial in advancing my career and enhancing my business knowledge. My time in audit included investigating a number of strange happenings, like this one:

It was in the 1970s and the company was in the process of replacing the black and white televisions with colour sets in the bedrooms of all of its four-star hotels.

Clive was the hotel manager in the only four-star hotel still to be upgraded. For over a month, he'd been chasing the company's central purchasing department to have the televisions changed, pointing out his hotel was now the only one left with black and white TVs.

Two days after his call to the purchasing department demanding his televisions be changed to colour, two vans pulled up outside the hotel and four men arrived to start the changeover. Clive was somewhat surprised by the speed of his request being processed by the purchasing department. It had been a much faster response than usual but he was exceptionally pleased it was going to be done.

The four men were in Radio Rental white overalls and the vans were also clearly marked 'Radio Rentals' (the large TV hire company). They went to the head porter, handed him a document, and explained they were here to replace the black and white televisions with colour ones. The head porter phoned

Clive's office to check and Clive confirmed they were expecting the exchange of televisions.

The changeover started and, with the help of a couple of porters, they loaded eighty-three black and white television sets into the two white vans within an hour.

Later that day, about five o'clock in the afternoon, the housekeeper went to Clive asking when the new colour televisions were to arrive. She'd been told that morning by the men who took the old black and white TVs that they were going to bring the new colour TVs early in the afternoon.

At this point, one of Clive's assistant managers phoned central purchasing to chase up the delivery, only to be told they knew nothing about new televisions for the hotel. Clive then phoned the central purchasing manager, who confirmed what his assistant manager had been told: the order hadn't yet been processed for the colour televisions. It appeared a bold scam had taken place and the black and white TVs had in fact been stolen.

At this point, I became involved in the investigation. The police interviewed the head porter, housekeeper and other staff who'd opened doors for the fake Radio Rentals men, helped them carry the televisions to the vans and even given them tea and biscuits in the staff room.

The paperwork initially presented to the head porter for the removal of the televisions was missing. Evidently, they'd shown a paper authorising removal and replacement of the televisions, but said they would get it signed and leave it with the head porter when they knew exactly how many televisions were put in the vans.

The police checked with Radio Rentals to discover they didn't have that type of van, nor did they recognise the descriptions of any of the men. Neither the men nor the TVs were ever found.

It took the company three days to replace the missing

black and white televisions with, of course, new colour ones. I remember Clive saying, "Although the theft was unfortunate and exceptionally bold, I did receive the new colour televisions in record time."

Computer Hacking – an Early Case

I started working in hotels in the 1960s, when all reservations systems were based on paper or pin boards. In most hotels of up to fifty rooms, billing was done in a paper, manual, tabular ledger. The most technical support was from mechanical billing and accounting machines. Computers were just starting to be introduced.

The first real computer system I remember for purchasing and sales involved punch cards. Next was a very large, delicate machine housed at head office, in a clean, thermostatically controlled room, connected through the telephone system to each hotel. It was affectionately called 'Chris' (Central Hotels Reservations Information System).

Chris was not like a modern system. We had to input a code for our hotel, add the type and number of rooms wanted, the arrival and departure date and a code instead of a name. The receptionist making the booking kept a paper copy of the entry, added the booking code to the paper booking details and filed it in alphabetical order under the day of arrival.

Every morning at 3am, Chris would print the arrivals list for the next two days for all twenty London hotels, along with a listing of room availability for the next four weeks, and any days fully booked in the future. This allowed the receptionist to book small numbers of rooms well into the future. Larger bookings would always be sent to the company's central booking office.

Our managing director, having spent half a million pounds

on the system, was almost fanatical about it being used, and would go round the hotels checking receptionists were using it exclusively and not keeping back-ups in the form of paper room-density charts.

Like most new computer systems, there were occasional problems, but, in general, it did provide head office, and in particular the sales department, with a very clear picture of the whole company's room availability, and in doing this, ensured the company's hotels were nearly always full.

Its demise was due to an unfortunate incident in one of the hotels. George, a night manager, had an argument with his manager and subsequently handed in his resignation to the hotel personnel department, giving one month's notice.

On arriving at work the following evening, George found the hotel's general manager waiting for him, and, after a brief meeting, the manager informed George that he was to pack his belongings and leave in the morning after his night shift.

That night, George went to work on the computer system and fully booked every hotel in the group for eleven years using codes only he knew. At the end of his shift in the morning, he picked up his outstanding wages and left, never to be seen again.

It was two days before the listings came out and chaos started. The computer system was shut down, never to be used again, and every hotel reception manager pulled out the old, hidden room-density charts and it was back to the manual system for another couple of years.

We could never prove it was George as the codes used were appropriate to each hotel, but at the time these were very easy to get as they came with every night's printouts. As the London hotel scene is fairly small, sometime later I met a friend of George's, who told me how he had done it and that George was now working in the computer industry.

Making a Snowman from the Microwave

This is a story resulting from a lack of training. In this hotel, the kitchen staff would prepare and leave food out on metal trays for the night staff. The night staff would heat up the food and have their night meal in the early morning.

The hotel had just installed microwaves. As usual, the kitchen staff had left out food for the night staff in a metal tray in the fridge, with a note instructing them to place their meals on plates and heat them up in the microwave for two minutes.

I was duty manager and just finishing off in the office when the head night porter came running into my office to report a small fire in the kitchen. I ran with him into the restaurant kitchen, where one of the night porters was standing by the microwave spurting out profuse acrid smoke from the burning plastic inside.

When I saw the fire extinguisher in his hand, I shouted to him not to open the microwave door. Too late, he did so and the flames leapt out at him. He responded immediately by setting off the extinguisher, pointing it directly into the open microwave.

Well, did he get a fright? The foam hit the back of the small microwave and returned with a vengeance, totally covering him from the waist up in the thick, white stuff. He really did look like a snowman.

It appears this night porter put the metal dish in the oven, not knowing what the consequences would be. Next day, a notice went up on all the remaining microwaves, 'No metal dishes or cutlery to be put in this oven'.

Police Vigilance

Speaking of electronics reminds me of an operation carried out by the London Hotel Police Squad in the early 1970s. Their task was to reduce hotel fraud and theft from bedrooms. In my experience, they did a great job in reducing hotel theft and other crimes.

At this time, the older hotels tended not to have very secure bedroom door locking systems, and a good shoulder push would open most guest doors. This all changed with the fitting of new fire doors, along with better door frames and locks.

The hotel in question was having a spate of night time burglaries. Four or five rooms on a floor would be forced open, often while people were sleeping in the room. Once entered, the rooms were carefully ransacked of small valuables and cash.

After one of these night time robberies, a guest reported having been disturbed by someone banging on their door. They had shouted, "Who is it?" and the reply from outside the door was, "Night porter cleaning shoes, sorry for disturbing you, sir, I dropped one."

At that time, if you left shoes outside your room, they were polished by the night porters; this service was stopped in our hotels due to numerous pranks by guests, who would change the shoes around and in one case, someone actually collected them all and put them down the rubbish chute. This took ages to sort out, and generated a great deal of complaints from irate customers and, surprisingly, after the guests had collected their footwear, we were one shoe over.

Anyway, back to the robberies. The police had a plan. One evening, they turned up about nine o'clock and installed five miniature microphones, one on each floor. These were radio-linked to a receiver in the manager's office, the police base for the night.

It was just after two o'clock in the morning when one of the microphones picked up banging on the 5th floor. The three officers rushed out of the office up to the 5th floor, one in each lift and the third taking the main staircase. After searching for ten minutes, they found nothing and made their way back down to the office, only to find their somewhat expensive radio receiver missing. They checked the hotel from top to bottom but found nothing, so left somewhat embarrassed to return to the police station and explain the theft of the equipment to their superintendent.

At the time, we all reckoned it was an inside job, but in the morning, as the guests were checking out, a very observant hall porter noticed one of our regular guests was leaving carrying a case he didn't arrive with. The police were called while the guest was delayed at the checkout.

As he was about to exit the hotel, two police officers approached him and took him away. He was later charged with theft from several hotels. At his trial, he confessed to visiting over thirty hotels in London in the last year, some as many as eight times, and carried out over three hundred thefts from bedrooms. He spent the next year and some months in just one hotel, Her Majesty's prison.

Oh yes, the observant porter? He received a large financial reward from the court and a bonus from the company. You see, it pays to keep your eyes open.

Mystery Shopper Reports

There are many stories not included in this book, mainly because of their unpleasant nature. This book is about the incidents that made me smile, like this one:

Most hotel companies employ agencies to check on the quality of their hotels, and reports on their visits are sent back to the company's directors, similar to mystery shoppers in retail premises. Usually, a copy of the report would arrive at the hotel manager's desk about two weeks after the stay. The report would have a number of points underlined, to be addressed or requiring an explanation in writing to the directors.

Sometimes, the reports were very helpful in identifying minor fraud or poor service. On this particular occasion, I read a report in which there was only one paragraph underlined for comment.

The mystery guest had booked by telephone, arrived at the hotel, been welcomed by the receptionist, and provided with a room which was perfectly serviced, with all the equipment working and up to standard. He had a restaurant meal, described as 'well-cooked' and served by friendly and efficient staff. After dinner, he went to the bar, leaving when it shut, on time, and made his way back to his room.

However, he didn't take the lift. Instead, he checked all the fire staircases and exits where, to his surprise, he came across a couple making love at the basement exit. This was the bit underlined and with a comment from the director requesting me to 'Please check and tell me what you are going to do'.

I responded as follows:

'I thought they must have finished by now but I did check and they were not there'.

'It is now twelve days since he came across the couple. Perhaps you could ask him why he did not report the incident to the staff at the time or did he just stay and watch?'

I got no response to my comments. I wonder why?

The Mouse that Came for Breakfast

I was reminded of this event only recently by a friend who stayed at this very hotel and was praising it for its luxury and excellent service.

Being a station hotel in the West End of London, breakfast started early at 6am. It was served in the large, spacious main restaurant at the east end of the ground floor. Despite opening at 6am, the actual number of guests seeking breakfast at that time was few. Breakfast trade really took off at about 7am. Until then, the restaurant was normally very quiet with a few customers, and fewer staff.

As duty manager, I started at 6.30am, doing the changeover with the night manager over a leisurely, early breakfast. As normal, we sat at a table near the door, where we could see almost everything happening in the restaurant and keep an eye on the hotel reception area.

During a lull in our conversation, I looked round the restaurant and noticed a waiter on his route to the kitchen. He veered off the main centre aisle and swung his leg, as if to kick the table occupied by an elderly businessman, who was totally absorbed in reading his paper.

A couple of minutes later, another waiter came down the aisle carrying a tray, and he also swerved off to the same table and appeared to kick out at the table, while the customer was still totally oblivious to what was happening. I decided to move my chair a little for a better view. It took me a couple of seconds to focus on what it was they were trying to kick… a mouse! It appeared to be quite content sitting up against the gentleman's shoe, looking out across the restaurant.

The first waiter returned and, once again, he walked over to the table and out shot his foot to kick the mouse, but this time I noticed the mouse appeared to duck its head out of the way of the oncoming foot and watched as the waiter stumbled on to the kitchen.

By now, my colleague and I were totally mesmerised by the mouse as it ducked another half dozen kicks aimed at him, before a bright waiter casually dropped a tray at the back of the table, sending the mouse scurrying across the restaurant, and causing the customer to jump out of his chair and spill his coffee with fright.

The elderly businessman never knew of his table guest, and later that day the pest control people arrived and cleared the area of the wee timorous beasties.

Betty and the Conservative Dinner

Betty was a wonderful Scottish lady in the later part of middle age; a fantastic worker with a real individualist personality. She was what we called a 'jobbing waitress', a waitress from a pool of casual waiting staff paid by the hour, to serve at functions or in one of the hotel restaurants.

She was always dressed in a smart black dress with a crisp, well-starched white apron, but the individual aspect of Betty's dress was that her blouse sleeves always had bright blue elasticated cuffs.

The first time Betty came to my attention was at a Scottish Conservative Party dinner. It was the grand finale event of their annual conference, at a time when they had many Scottish MPs and councillors. The dinner was being attended by about three hundred supporters from across the country, with a top table of dignitaries from both Houses of Parliament. It was a silver service meal and the main course was, somewhat unusually for the time, chicken served with a vegetable of creamed spinach.

The dinner was in full flow and the conversation lively and loud. Hilda, the banqueting manager, and I were stationed behind the top table to ensure everything was operating smoothly, when a senior parliamentary cabinet minister turned to get my attention. I went over and he said, "The spinach is wonderful, any chance of a little more?" Hilda also heard his request and walked quickly down to the other end of the hall where she had found Betty serving spinach.

Hilda whispered to her, "One of the dignitaries on the top table wants more spinach." So off marched Betty to the top table, but instead of walking behind the seated guests, she walked along the front of the table with the spinach salver outstretched for the guests to see, hoping the requester would notice and signal to her.

After crossing the table twice without being noticed, she stood facing the middle of the table and in her loud Scottish accent addressed the top table with, "Okay Popeye, where are you?" At this point, the top table and those nearby went into hysterical laughter, while a very embarrassed cabinet minister put up his hand like a naughty little school boy.

He even got a mention as Popeye, the strong man, in the after dinner speeches, and it certainly livened up the dinner.

Betty and the Welsh

Rugby between the Welsh and Scots has always been not merely a great competitive event but a huge social occasion for the Celts. In the 1970s, our hotel in Edinburgh would be completely full for the week, from the Sunday before the match to the Sunday after. To cope with demand for alcohol, we kept at least one of the hotel's three bars open for residents twenty-four hours a day during their stay.

The Welsh guys came from the valleys' miners' working clubs. They would save up for the two years between the away matches and come in coaches for a week's holiday, climaxing with the match. It was normal for only about half of them to have tickets for the match. The rest would watch in the pubs all over Edinburgh.

This happened on a Monday evening at the beginning of the week. Betty was serving a group of the lads in the restaurant when one of them asked her if she knew of a pub where they could have a good time. Betty explained that at her age, a good time was a night in front of the television with a cup of tea, hardly what these lads were looking for, but she popped into the kitchen to ask the young chefs if they had any ideas of places where the Welshmen could have a good night.

A couple of minutes later, she returned with a smile on her face, and began to tell the boys of the chefs' suggestions.

"The chefs gave me three suggestions because they weren't sure what sort of evening you were looking for. If it's a good beer drinking pub you are looking for, then the Gravediggers is what you want. If it's a music singing pub then the Captain's Bar is a great place, but if it's just a leg over you want, then you'll get that at the Trash Bar."

At this point, the lads, along with the rest of the restaurant, both customers and staff, went into fits of laughter. Betty, now feeling very embarrassed, retreated to the kitchen where the chefs, once they'd stopped laughing, explained a 'leg over' was not a type of beer as Betty had thought.

Betty was so mortified by her restaurant confrontation that she signed off sick for the rest of the week, too embarrassed to come in.

A Bird in the Bag

At the time of this story, I was working and living with my wife, baby daughter and two dogs in a Scottish City Hotel with a flat on the fifth floor. At this time, my hobby was rough shooting. I would go out with friends hunting, mainly feathered game, which was taken back to the hotel as food for the guests. I was part of a little shooting syndicate where we acted as gamekeepers for a 1,000 acre estate.

On this day, two of us were out early to work on the estate, and spent a couple of hours shooting before returning home rather later than expected. On arrival back at the hotel, John, my shooting companion for the day, took the shot game to the hotel kitchen, while I hurried up to the flat to change out of my shooting clothes, dump my shooting bag and change into my dinner suit for evening duty.

The evening dinner service was going well when a receptionist called to tell me my wife desperately needed to speak to me. I phoned up to the flat and when she answered, I could hear the dogs barking before she shouted to me, "Get up here now!"

Fearing something dreadful, I rushed upstairs and, on opening the door, was met with chaos. Our two spaniels were rushing around barking, jumping over the furniture chasing a partridge, which was flying from room to room trying to evade the dogs and find a way out. Adding to this, my wife had a squash racket in hand, trying to get to the bird while avoiding the dogs and furniture.

It took me a couple of seconds to decide whether I should open the window and let the injured bird possibly escape or take the squash racket and end the poor creature's life.

I grabbed the dogs and shut them out of the room. At this, my wife and the bird calmed down and I was able to catch the partridge in a blanket and put it out of its pain.

My wife was certainly not a happy lady. The flat was in a mess, the dogs and bird had been all over the furniture, the poor bird had pooed everywhere and the baby was still venting her screams from the kitchen.

Was I getting hell? Yes! And:

Why hadn't I made sure the game bag was empty? And, more importantly:

Why had I not checked the bird was dead?

Well, I quickly made my escape and left the flat with the excuse that I was needed at work, while my somewhat distressed wife cooled down.

Did this have any lasting effect? Well YES, my daughter is still petrified of birds and guess who's to blame for all of this? Me, of course, and rightly too, for which I apologise – but who opened the bag? Not me.

First Time Flying

I've worked with some fabulous people, and this story is about two in particular, Susan and Mary, who were responsible for cleaning the hotel areas. They were both always chirpy and a pleasure to meet in the morning.

Susan was a vibrant lady in her early thirties, who holidayed for a week every year in Majorca with her family. Mary was in her late fifties, and had spent the last fifteen years holidaying with her husband George in a small cottage just ten miles away. Mary and George had never been more than fifty miles from home, and certainly never on an aeroplane.

I remember Mary coming to tell me her exciting news. She and George had been persuaded by the stories from Susan and her own niece to holiday in Majorca this year. They were going to join her niece and family in Majorca for a holiday. She'd been down to the local travel agent, it was all booked, and she was so excited about the whole thing.

It was a couple of days later that Susan came into my office, giggling profusely, to tell me this story.

Susan's tale to me, in between spasms of laughter

It started last week when Mary and I were having our early morning cuppa. She told me she'd been down to the travel agent and booked the holiday, with flights from Glasgow Airport to Majorca. We chatted on and I told her of all the great places to go and how she was going to have a fantastic time.

She told me how much she and George were looking forward

to the holiday, and how they were just a little bit worried about the flying, because they'd never been on a plane. I told her not to worry, flying was easy, but then I just had a devilish idea and casually asked, "Do either of you have false teeth?" and she told me they both did.

I explained it wouldn't be a problem; they just had to remember before take-off and landing to remove their false teeth and put them in the paper bag provided. The bags would be in the pouch on the back of the seat in front of them. Mary asked me, "Why?" I told her, "The air pressure inside the cabin can change quite suddenly during take-off and landing, and false teeth sometimes just fly out of your mouth. For safety and to save any embarrassment, they supply these bags for people to discreetly put their false teeth in."

I thought no more of it, until yesterday when Mary came into work and let fly at me, saying she'd never been so embarrassed and humiliated in all her life, and was never ever going to speak to me again, and stormed out of the room, not even having tea. Well, I had no idea what she was on about, but this morning I told her we had been friends for years and whatever I had done to upset her, I was really sorry. Mary had obviously calmed down a bit and started to tell me what happened to cause her upset.

The story Mary told Susan that morning.

The day after we had the conversation about flying and false teeth, I went down town to the travel agent where I had booked the holiday, wanting to speak to the nice girl I had booked the holiday with. The place was busy and I waited until she was free. I approached her desk, asking if she remembered me, and the girl said, "Yes," and asked me if there was a problem with the booking.

Well, I said, "I'm not that worried about flying, but my husband George is a bit embarrassed about having to take his false teeth out and put them in the bag, and wants to know how he'll be able to eat on the plane without his teeth?"

The assistant was looking at me a bit funny and said, "Worried about taking his teeth out?" "Yes," I said, "Susan from work, who flies to Majorca quite often, told me the change in cabin pressure on take-off causes people's false teeth to fly out of their mouth, and where to find the paper bag to put them in." At this point the assistant started grinning and said, "No, no, no." Then she started laughing, along with most of the people in the shop.

It was then I realised that you'd made a complete fool of me and in front of all those people. I rushed out of the shop vowing to get that ****** Susan! You bitch!

Susan continued

I just had to laugh and in the end the two of us were in fits of laughter and friends again. I'm just so glad she eventually saw the funny side of it.

And back to me

I have to say I also found the story hilarious, and later, when I spoke to Mary, she told me she would bide her time and get her own back on the bitch. The moral of the story… never laugh too loud at others as you may well be the butt of the next joke.

Mary's Revenge

Susan, the cause of so much embarrassment to Mary over the false teeth incident, had for three years been taking driving lessons and failed the test at least eight times, mainly due to her poor use of gears and lack of traffic awareness.

It was now a year after Susan's prank with the false teeth. A new large and expensive multipurpose floor polisher had arrived in the hotel. I'm not sure what inspired Mary to set this up but I presume it was Susan's nervousness around machines. Anyway, as soon as it had arrived, Mary set to work to plan her revenge, with the help of Bert, the service engineer.

The service engineer added a fake gear stick to the handle of the polisher, just under the on/off switch, with positions marked 'reverse' and 'forward'. He called Susan to his office and told her she was to be given this expensive and complex new machine, but before handing it over, he needed to see her driving licence to be assured she was suitably qualified, eligible and safe to use it.

Shyly, she explained she only had a provisional licence. He told her not to worry, but she would need to have some training and take a competency test before being able to use it without supervision.

A couple of days later, Susan arrived for her lesson with Bert, the engineer. He explained that, depending on how well she got on, they could probably do the test straight after the lesson. They went down to the large conference hall where an obstacle course made up of cones had been set up, and in the middle of the room was the large polishing machine with an L plate on the front. As they entered the room, he handed her a white coat with an 'L' stuck on the back, telling her once she passed the test, the Ls would be removed.

He explained the complexities of the new machine, the types of polisher and cleaner heads and what each was used for, followed by demonstrating how they were fitted. Then he described how the gears were used to increase speed and pressure of the cleaning brushes and pads. Susan spent the next half hour going round the obstacle course, changing gear from forward to reverse as appropriate. After a short while, she and Bert agreed she was ready to take the test.

The test involved setting up the machine, putting on the scrubbers, then taking them off, and fitting the soft polishers, before going round the circuit twice without hitting any of the obstacles, but polishing as close to them as possible.

On successfully completing the tasks, Bert congratulated her on passing her test. It was then Mary entered the room with Susan's certificate and a framed photograph of her in her white coat taking the test. Susan gasped before seeing the funny side of it and just roared with laughter!

What Susan didn't realise was that whilst all this had been going on, the rest of the cleaning staff and Susan's family had been sitting upstairs watching her on the large conference screen, needless to say in fits of laughter.

The Customer is Always Right

There are people with total belief in themselves who are never wrong, unable to accept they may have made a mistake. This is a story of one of these people.

The company had just purchased this budget hotel on the outskirts of a popular tourist city and I was sent to manage the takeover and assist the new manager with company procedures.

It had been raining all day. The evening rush was over and the head receptionist had gone home. Julie was the duty receptionist at the front office and I was going through the next day's booking in the back office. My concentration was broken by a lady having what appeared to be an argument with Julie at the front desk. I decided to find out what the problem was and see how I could help.

On entering the front office, I was confronted by two ladies at the desk. The older of the two, on seeing me enter, turned and in a very loud and high-pitched voice said, "You must be the manager. I think it's a disgrace you haven't even told your staff the hotel has been taken over, and you still have the old sign outside. What sort of company is this?"

Somewhat perplexed, I asked Julie what the problem was, but before she could even speak, the lady interrupted, "We have two rooms booked here and you've lost the booking, no doubt mislaid in the takeover."

Julie just looked at me and said, "We have no booking for these ladies. I've been through all today's bookings, checking both ladies' names, and I even checked the rest of the month's bookings."

I had to defuse the situation away from the desk, so I asked the ladies to take a seat at the far end of the reception area and joined them. The older lady never stopped talking, going on about what a disaster this was. She and her marketing manager were here at the hotel to attend the national conference and pick up a special award.

It was then it hit me. We had no conference suite! She was at the wrong hotel. I interrupted, saying, "You're booked in at the Cleveland Hotel for the National Marketing Awards?" To which the younger of the two ladies managed to say, "Yes, that's right," before the older lady said, "Why else would we be here?" I replied, "Well, the Cleveland Hotel is about five hundred yards from here. I think you must have taken the first turning left off the dual carriageway instead of the second."

"Well, you could have told us that earlier, and the sign at the end of the road did say the hotel was this way." Not wishing to cause any more concern, I apologised for the inconvenience and wished them well at the awards ceremony.

As I was following them out, the young lady dropped back and said, "I told her before we came in it was the wrong hotel but she wouldn't have it, saying it was your sign outside that was wrong."

It is My Dinner

Being always right is a characteristic definitely not restricted to a few women. In my time, I've probably found more men with this characteristic and this story is of one of them. Every year, the hotel would host a number of ladies' nights for the Round Table, Rotary Club, local sailing clubs, charity groups and other worthy organisations.

At this time, these events were always black tie and very formal until after the speeches, when the guests would retire to the bar for refreshments before working off their dinner elegantly, or not so, on the dance floor.

It started when the chairman of this particular organisation arrived to arrange the annual ladies' evening dinner dance. He was a large eloquent gentleman in his early sixties. He arrived with his wife, a lady of equal stature. We sat down and reviewed the previous year's event in order to decide on this year's menu. He was delighted with the format of the event, and wanted no change. He and his wife agreed that the dinner wine had been liked and they didn't wish to change that either. Then came the menu.

"Ah yes," he said, "my good lady wife and I have been in this club over thirty years and in all that time we've never really enjoyed any of the annual dinners. You see, the food isn't really what most people enjoy; you know, all this posh fancy food? We like good wholesome grub and, at last, now that I'm chairman, I get to choose the menu."

My heart stopped for a second. What on earth was this man

going to want? He continued, “The wife and I have decided what the menu is to be.” At that, he handed me the menu below.

To start: Scotch Broth Soup with soft white baps
Followed by: Deep Fried Scampi, tartar sauce with brown bread and butter
Main Course: Steak and Kidney Suet Pudding with roast and mashed potatoes, cabbage and carrots
Dessert: Spotted Dick with Custard
Cheese: Cheese Board and Coffee.

My worst thoughts had been realised. He and his wife might love this but I was sure the majority of the 150 expected guests wouldn't consider it an appropriate evening dinner. Worse, they would assume the hotel had chosen the menu.

Decision time!

Do I tell him this was not a suitable menu for a formal, annual, ladies' evening dinner dance? No!

I did discuss changing the main course to roast beef but his mind was made up. He was adamant. The guests would all love this meal and he knew this because many of them had eaten the same meal at his house. He was adamant this year's dinner was going to be the best in thirty years, a real meal, and everyone would love it.

Thinking on my feet and not wishing to lose this very lucrative event, or have our reputation for special dinner functions ruined, I agreed to his menu and, as a bonus, I offered to have the dinner menus printed here in the hotel at no extra cost. They left delighted. I knew it would have been useless to suggest an alternative menu as he was determined to have his menu for the dinner.

Later, discussing the event with the chef and the banqueting manager, we decided to offer a choice for each course on the menu.

So alongside his menu was: cream of mushroom soup –

smoked salmon with prawns – chicken breast in a lemon cream sauce and crème brûlée for the sweet.

On the evening of the dinner, I was worried the chairman could be upset by the hotel offering an alternative to his menu. In the hopes of alleviating this probability, at the reception I spoke with a couple of his special guests that I knew and explained what I had done and why. It was reassuring to hear they agreed the alternative menu would be more acceptable.

I was glad the chairman was kept fully engaged meeting and greeting his guests before the dinner. It wasn't until after the dinner I was able to meet with him and ask if he enjoyed the meal. He replied, "Best meal ever and I've spoken to a good few of the guests and they loved MY idea of offering a choice this year."

"I'm so pleased it went well," I replied, not wishing to take the glory from him but pleased to know the meal went well and the hotel would secure the booking next year.

After the meal, on analysis, we sold twelve of his main courses and 136 of ours, and everybody had a fantastic evening.

Yes! The customer is always right, or at least they should believe they are.

Children's Honesty

I often spent time at the cash desk in the morning when guests were checking out to wish departing guests a safe journey and answer any queries.

On this morning, a young lad about five years old was at the checkout desk with his dad. It was all very normal. His father was going through the bill, querying a couple of items and having them explained to his satisfaction.

As he came to the end and was about to pay, the young lad, who was sitting on the checkout desk, asked the cashier if the towel and glasses Daddy had in his case were on the bill. He went on to tell her Daddy liked them so much he was going to take them home for Mummy.

The father blushed like beetroot and the little boy started to laugh, while the cashier turned and looked at me. I walked over and, before I could say a word, he said, "OK, sorry, I have them in my case, how much?"

I asked him to come into my office where he opened his case and, sure enough, there were two bar glasses wrapped in a hotel towel. Did he buy them? No. I gave him a lecture on theft – yes, in front of his son, and he left without the stolen goods.

Should I have let him pay and keep them? I think not. Theft from hotels costs a fortune and I had no wish to endorse his actions. However, I bet he never took another thing when his son was with him.

The Blocked Drain

You can imagine the amount of grease a busy hotel kitchen generates. The majority goes down the sink but not directly into the sewer. Most catering establishments are required to have a grease trap to catch this unwanted gunk before it actually clogs up the sewers. These grease traps have to be replaced regularly by a specialist company, and this incident happened the morning after our grease trap had been serviced.

The hotel had two small banqueting suites, one on the ground floor and one in the basement alongside the banqueting kitchen. At about nine o'clock on the Saturday morning, the kitchen porter came to tell me water was creeping out from under the kitchen door into the basement banqueting area. I rushed down to see what was leaking, to find that the water was, in fact, not coming from the kitchen but from the beer cellar situated at the other side of the kitchen.

The beer cellar was situated in a small square open area, with a floor about four inches below the level of the kitchen. I crossed the kitchen, opened the door and looked down into about four inches of sewage water bubbling out of the manhole cover just inside the cellar. The four inches of dirty water filled the cellar to the level of the kitchen, and was now flowing across the kitchen out to the banqueting reception area, where the carpet was sodden and smelly.

I guessed the sewage pipe was blocked and the chef told me a drain company had been in the day before changing the grease traps. It took only a few minutes to phone them, and they arrived within half an hour. In the meantime, we placed wooden boards and tabletops on the carpets to walk on above the ever seeping sewage. Ten minutes after arriving, the man from the drain company came to tell me he'd found and fixed the problem. It was a torch. One of the men from the day before must have dropped it down the drain.

As he was telling me this, the chef phoned from the kitchen to tell me the barman had fallen down the open manhole in the beer cellar. He'd managed to get the barman out but he'd definitely hurt himself. The drain man and I ran down to the basement, both slipping on the wooden planks and falling into the sewage, which now covered the lower reception area.

Now wet and smelly, I called an ambulance for the barman, who'd swallowed a fair mouthful of sewage on descending the manhole. He returned to work a few weeks later, after being treated in hospital and having time off to heal his injured back.

That afternoon, the reception area had new carpets fitted and a specialist cleaning company cleaned the whole basement area. Sometime later, I was given a new suit by the drain company and the barman received a handsome compensation package, and… we did manage to serve a banquet that evening.

The £500 VPO

Visitor Paid Out (VPO) is a practice used in some hotels. It involves the hotel paying and billing guests for goods and services that are not part of the hotel business. These could include taxi fares, tours, theatre tickets booked by the hotel, and goods delivered to the hotel for guests. For special customers, it could be more.

This incident took place in the 1970s before we all had debit and credit cards and VPOs were common practice. It happened in a large London hotel, involving a regular customer who, for over five years, stayed at the hotel once a month for between three and seven days. He was always polite, very friendly with staff and renowned for giving large financial tips for their service.

It started when I was undertaking one of my regular duties of checking guests' accounts. I noticed an outstanding account for a room, where the occupants should have checked out four days previously. This was ringing alarm bells to me, a guest leaving without paying his bill. Therefore, I started to check the bill in detail and to my horror there was a £500 VPO, and, even more alarming, a petty cash voucher indicating he'd received £500 in cash.

All of this was totally against company policy, a VPO for cash, signed by the customer and the chief cashier (basically an IOU).

Immediately, I called a meeting with the head cashier and the hotel accountant. The cashier explained this had been going on for a few years and the man always paid his bill before leaving, and would add a hundred pound tip (a huge amount at the time) for the front office staff.

I asked if anyone had seen the man since the evening he had collected his £500 VPO. "No" was the answer. I checked to see if he actually had left his room, to find his clothes and personal belongings still there. I had the room emptied, door lock changed and his belongings packed and put in safe storage, with instructions for them only to be returned on full payment of the outstanding account.

Could we contact the gentleman? We checked his registration to find an address in Switzerland but no telephone number. We managed to find a telephone number through the international operator and phoned several times. Each time, an answer phone stated the gentleman was away on business and requested us to leave a message, which we did every day for the next three weeks without success. Out of desperation, we even wrote to the gentleman enclosing his bill and requesting immediate payment, but again no response. After four weeks, the bill was sent to our head office as an unpaid account. In addition, the head cashier was made to pay the £500 VPO and received a formal written final warning, although I was sure he would never do it again.

I thought that was the end of the incident until about four weeks later, when two plain clothed police officers arrived at the hotel wanting to see me. In my office, they showed me a picture of a man they thought had been staying in the hotel. Not being sure if it was our missing guest, I asked for the head cashier to come up to the office. He confirmed the identity and told them that the gentleman had gone out on his last evening at the hotel to a local gambling club.

The police said they knew that, and, after an hour's questioning, they thanked us. As they were about to leave, I mentioned the outstanding bill for £1,700.

They explained that getting our money back was very unlikely as the man was in fact an international arms dealer of some repute who was now dead. He'd been shot on the night he left the hotel and found in the River Thames a week later.

A Memo from Head Office

I remember one Saturday evening when I was managing a hotel with four banqueting suites in the north of Britain, far away from the company's head office in London. The evening was very busy, with four weddings, one in each of the banqueting suites.

A member of the bar staff radioed for help. I rushed up the grand staircase from my office on the ground floor, to find a noisy confrontation on the landing between the first and second floors.

The altercation was between a guest from the reception on floor one and a guest from the reception on the second floor. By the time I arrived, several guests from each wedding had started to join in, and our security officers were trying to separate them and send them back to their respective reception areas.

I asked the guests to return to their parties but kept back the two main protagonists, telling them to cool down and pointing out that if there was any more trouble, they would have to leave. All of a sudden, they flew at each other and, as I was in between them, I grabbed each at arm's length to hold them apart. In turn, they grabbed the sleeves of my jacket, resulting in it splitting right up the back. Before long, the security officers stepped in and escorted the gentlemen out of the building.

Having had my dinner suit jacket torn in half in the line of duty, I sent an insurance claim for a new one to head office. Ten days later, imagine my surprise when I received a memo from the operations director which read, 'On this occasion, the company has agreed to reimburse the cost of the dinner suit jacket. However, might I suggest that in future you divest yourself of your outer garments before diving into the fray?'

Can you imagine it, me asking these two guys to wait a minute before fighting while I removed my jacket just in case it got torn? He obviously had never been in such a situation.

A Present for a New Home

This occurred in a large city centre hotel with a popular soundproofed basement disco, where four hundred souls could dance away till the early hours. The entrance to the disco was around the corner and a fair distance from the main hotel entrance. The entrance to the disco itself was a narrow corridor about two metres wide, with a rail down the middle monitored constantly by at least two doormen.

It was early December, a cold, crisp evening. I was still on duty, supervising the end of a large function as the clock approached 2am, when I was approached by the disco manager. He told me the eight-foot Christmas tree with all its baubles and lights had disappeared from the disco and he couldn't understand how on earth they could have taken it out. Having finished with the banquet, I went with him down the staff staircase to the disco.

It was simple to see from the trail of Christmas tree needles that it had left through the main door. What was not so clear was how they got it past the four door staff.

On returning to my office, I contacted the police, just in case it was spotted being carried down the road, as it was far too big to fit in a car. I entered the theft into the manager's logbook. Duty done, I sleepily sauntered off to the lift to my room on the 6th floor. Guess my surprise when entering the lift, I found the floor covered in Christmas tree needles. Surely not? How could they get it in through the front hall without being noticed by the numerous staff and guests? I contacted the night manager and together we followed the trail from the lift along the third floor corridor to a bedroom door. We knocked on the door and it was opened by a very drunk young lady.

We identified ourselves and, through the open door, could see the Christmas tree standing in the corner of the room. Questioning this very inebriated young lady was proving a waste of time, as she had no idea where it came from or how it got there. So we left with the tree and arranged to meet her and her roommate in the morning.

In the morning, the disco manager and I met with the lady, the bride from the hen party that had been at the disco the previous night. She and her roommate (who on our visit to their room the previous night had been dead to the world) knew nothing about how the tree got there and they were certainly not strong enough to have carried it there themselves. End of story, I thought.

However, the young ladies, on returning from a late breakfast an hour later, came to my office and handed me a note they'd found in the corner of room where the Christmas tree had been. It read, 'Every new home at Christmas needs a tree. Wishing you the best on your wedding, signed the Christmas fairies'.

We never did find out how it got there without being seen, but if you are one of the Christmas fairies perhaps you could let me know.

Children

Happy children in hotels contribute greatly to the enjoyment and satisfaction of the parents' holiday experience. For a few years, I worked in a family-friendly coastal hotel, which catered for children as a major element of the business during school summer holidays.

This story relates to a child's lost luggage. The child, who we shall call Mary, was about five years old and staying in the hotel for a couple of days with her father and brother John, aged about nine.

It was checking out time on Friday morning and the cash desk had its normal small queue of guests examining and paying their bills. Mary's father had just finished paying the account and was on his way with the children to the front door when the young girl suddenly realised that her little suitcase was missing and started to cry. The family moved back to the reception area where I was standing with the head porter. He explained Mary had left her small case somewhere and asked if we could help find it.

He asked Mary where she'd been since leaving the room with her case. Slowly her lip went down and the tears began to swell once more as, looking down at the floor, she said, "I went with Mummy to see Ben to thank him for being such a nice waiter."

"Did you leave the case in the restaurant?" he asked.

"No, no. I know I left it in the nursery with Margaret while I was having a last ride on the swings. She'll look after Mummy."

I phoned down to the nursery and, a couple of minutes later, Margaret arrived with the little case. On her arrival, wee Mary again started to cry while sobbing, "Sorry, Mummy."

At this point, the father picked her up. Looking at me, he explained the children's mother had recently died and each of them had been taking it in turns to carry the ashes in their case, on the way north to have them interred.

Somewhat taken aback, I gave my condolences and wished them a safe journey.

The Ghostly Loo

This story happened to Jane (a night cleaner in the hotel) one November evening as she went down to the basement to clean the kitchen staff's changing room.

It was about 10.30pm. I'd just finished my late tour of the hotel. Arriving back at my office, I found Jane and Bill (the night manager) sitting waiting for me. Jane was obviously upset and I asked her to tell me in her own words what had happened.

Jane's story, without all the interruptions for sobs:

I've been doing this job 'ere for over five years and nothing ever happened to me like this before. I was so scared I near wet myself running along that basement corridor. As you know, I start work at ten and, if the kitchen staff has left, I tidy and clean up the changing rooms before sweeping and mopping the basement corridor.

Well, I went in the kitchen and turned on the light to go to my cleaning cupboard, when I heard someone in the toilet. I turned and looked in and there sitting on the toilet was a real ghost! It was white, with its head on its lap. I screamed and it stood up. Well, I was just so scared I ran out into the corridor and I could hear it behind me. I ran screaming to reception and into the office here to be with people. I thought it was coming to get me.

And back to me:

She was still absolutely shaking.

She continued:

Bill was here; he sat me down. I told him there was a ghost in the basement and it chased me from the kitchen. He left me with Debbie while he and one of the porters ran down to the kitchen but they didn't find it. I did see it, I really did, and it knew my name.

And back to me again:

Not being a real believer in ghosts, I left Jane with a cup of tea and even though Bill and one of the porters had already done this, I went with Bill to investigate in the basement and the kitchen. Sure enough, there was nothing out of the ordinary and no one there. A mystery, I just had to find out more but in the meantime, I put Jane to work with a buddy for the rest of the shift and left the kitchen cleaning to her colleagues.

The next morning, I interviewed a number of kitchen and cleaning staff and discovered there had been a story circulating the hotel since Halloween of a headless ghost who wandered the hotel. It was said to be the ghost of a duke beheaded on this site many hundreds of years ago, but I could find no one who had seen it or who was the originator of the story.

Later in the day, the head chef, Carl, who was on a day off came to see me. He said he had something to tell me about the incident with Jane.

Carl's story:

It started last month on Halloween Night in the pub after work. Frank, my assistant, asked if the hotel had a ghost and I made up the story of a headless phantom who roamed the basement. Then this week in town when I saw one of those full-size model heads, an idea came to me, and last night was an ideal opportunity.

Frank and I were last out of the kitchen and we went up to the public bar for a drink before I gave him a lift home. As we were leaving the bar, I told him I'd left the car keys in the changing room and was going to pop down and get them, knowing if I was more than a couple of minutes, he would come and chase me up. Once there, I put the sheet over me and sat on the loo with the model head on my lap, and waited for Frank.

Hearing someone enter, I assumed it was Frank so I moaned, but what a fright I got when Jane stood at the door and screamed at me. I jumped up, ran after her to try and explain and calm her down, but she just kept running.

I decided it would be better to disappear so I put the head and sheet in my bag and walked out through the staff door to meet Frank and go home. Honestly, boss, I never really thought it would have such an effect on poor Jane.

When Frank phoned me this morning to tell me what happened, I knew I had to come in and own up. I never meant to frighten poor Jane; it was just to be a laugh with Frank, who now actually believes there is a headless ghost."

I told him the seriousness of what he'd done and the effect it had on Jane, and suggested he come back at 10pm and meet up with Jane to apologise, after which I would decide on any disciplinary action.

Thankfully, Jane accepted his apology and his peace offering of chocolates and beer, but boy, did she let him have it! Well, that was the end of his ghost and pranks but I think Frank still believes there is a headless spectre.

DAILY
MAIL

My Last Senior Management Dinner

This was one of my last days as an employee in the hospitality industry. The company I was employed with had brought all senior managers and directors together for a two-day conference.

On day two of the conference, I had a telephone call in the morning confirming the purchase of my new enterprise. In the evening, the dinner was excellent and we were all expecting an after-dinner motivational speaker, or something similar. Instead, the chairman and operations director left, saying they had an important meeting to attend and were leaving us with the new vice-chairman.

That left us, about twenty managers along with the marketing and finance directors, in the hands of this rather pompous new vice-chairman, whose knowledge of hotels was, to say the least, limited.

Anyway, he stood up and told us the rest of the evening was going to be very informal, getting to know each other, and we should start it off with a joke session. Expressions of amazement went round the room. We all knew each other quite well, and the thought of the cost of bringing us all together for a joke session was not appreciated.

Things went from bad to worse. He started telling us South African, racist, Kaffir jokes, not funny, just plain embarrassing, and after twenty minutes of this, realising no one was laughing, he asked if anyone else had any jokes.

Sitting next to me was my old colleague Bob and, knowing

I'd spent some of my life writing jokes, asked if I could do something to bring it to an end.

I stood up and told a joke in total bad taste (for which I give my apologies now before you read it). To understand the joke, you need to know that our chairman was an Eastern European gentleman called Elliot, our operations director was an English man named John and the vice-chairman, who was telling the jokes, was a South African named Bert.

The joke:

Three gentlemen met at an international conference. Elliot was a wealthy Eastern European, John was a very well educated and clever businessman and Bert was an excellent talker.

Elliot said he had five million pounds and wanted to start a hotel company. John said he had five hundred thousand pounds, plus a lot of hotel experience, and would love to be involved. They both looked at Bert, who said, "Yeah, I'd love to be involved and I do have about five hundred pounds I could invest."

Elliot said that with his five million pounds, he wanted to be the chairman; John said he felt with his five hundred thousand pounds and experience, and he'd like to be operations director. They turned and looked at Bert, who asked, "What could I be with my five hundred pounds?"

Elliot and John looked at each other, then turned to him and said, "You can be the vice-chairman."

Bert smiled and asked, "What does a vice-chairman do?" In unison, they replied, "When we want your bloody advice, we'll ask for it!"

At this point, Bert stood up and left, while the rest of us had a good laugh and enjoyed a social evening without him.

Yes, I left a month later to start my new business and never did meet him again.

Request for Driving Lessons

I received a strange request from one of our pub regulars, Clive. He popped into the public bar early one Monday morning, ordered his normal pint of beer, but before picking it up and paying he wandered through to the other bar and the toilet. On his return he paid and asked if anyone else was in. I said, "No," as my wife and the chef were outside sorting the kitchen stores for the day.

He explained he didn't want anyone to know what he was going to say, as it was to be a present for his wife, who was a young, slim, blonde lady in her mid-thirties, about half his age.

"Okay, Clive," I said, "What is it?" He replied, "I want her to learn to drive." "Oh, that's good," I said enthusiastically, "Is she looking forward to learning to drive?" He explained that with her being a shy lady, she was more worried about who was going to be teaching her than actually learning to drive. She needed to have a teacher she would be comfortable with, and as she was comfortable with me, he asked if I would do it. He would pay me for my time and a small bonus when she passed her test.

I explained that I didn't really have the time and besides I would make a lousy driving instructor, to which he replied, "But she wants a baby as well!"

Taking a step back I said, "Clive, no disrespect, your Amy is a lovely lady, but I'm not the man to teach her to drive or help her have a baby," and with that, I walked into the other bar on the pretence of checking if anyone was there. When I returned a couple of seconds later, he had left.

We never spoke of it again but a year later she could drive and had a baby girl. I often wonder what the driving instructor's bonus was!

The Mouse and the Chef

Today, our environmental health officers do a great job of improving the hygiene standards of food storage, preparation rooms and cooking methods. This incident occurred when our kitchen and some of the adjoining rooms were being renovated.

It was the beginning of winter and the maintenance man, along with the pest control man, were going round the kitchen checking for holes and signs of mice. Suddenly, a wee field mouse jumped out of a cupboard and scampered across the kitchen to hide behind a corner cupboard.

On seeing the mouse, the chef grabbed a brush and chased after it to the cupboard it was hiding behind. He asked the maintenance man to pull out the cupboard, while he stood on one side with the brush and the pest control man on the other side with a shovel.

The mouse suddenly ran out in the direction of the chef, who swiftly brought the brush down. He missed the creature, but the mouse saw it as a means of escape, ran up the brush handle, then up the chef's arm inside his jacket and across his shoulders.

We all hurried over and started slapping him, while he wriggled and screamed. Eventually, the mouse fell out the bottom of his jacket, to be terminated by the pest control man.

We did laugh about it later and, yes, we all felt sorry for the poor little mouse, but not for the petrified chef.

VERM-
-X-

The Barmaid's Blush

It's customary to have a range of vending machines in pubs and hotels, although now the cigarette machines have all gone. There was a time not so long ago when nearly every bar sold cigarettes only through vending machines.

In one of our small lounge bars, the toilets were situated at the back of the room directly facing the bar. The barmaid, Brenda, watched as a young man, who had been sitting with his girlfriend, exited the gents' toilet and walked over to the bar counter. He quietly explained that he put his money in the machine but nothing had come out.

Brenda put her hand under the counter and discreetly handed the young man a packet of contraceptives. He opened his hand to look at what he had been given, "No, no, you're mistaken, it was the cigarette machine I lost my money in before I went to the loo, not the machine in the toilet." Brenda grabbed the packet back out of his hand and, seeing me entering, blurted out, "This young man has lost money in the cigarette machine," as she pushed past me, with her face bright red, to get away from her embarrassing situation.

You'll always find a policeman
(when you don't want one)

Picture the scene: it was mid-January, there was six inches of snow outside the pub, which was in the middle of a tiny village two miles off the main road. We'd had a very quiet night and it was 10.30pm, closing time. I was in the empty lounge bar painting the wall above the fireplace, when I heard a noise from the adjoining public bar. I walked round the central bar to find that our darts team had returned from an away game at a pub which had served beer not to their taste. They apologised for being late as they'd been delayed by the snow blizzard, which was still blowing. They asked, "Could we please have a quick beer before going home?"

I said, "Well, on this occasion OK, we're not likely to get caught for afterhours drinking," and started to serve them each a pint. We were chatting away when a commotion broke out next door in the lounge bar, where my Great Dane was barking aggressively. I ran through to find two policemen being held at the door by the dog. I called her back and apologised, while pointing out that we were closed.

Not moving from their position, backs to the door, the older policeman explained, "We're calling about the cars in the car park, just checking you weren't serving alcohol after permitted hours." Seeing they were a little nervous of the dog and rather anxious to leave, I lied. I told them that the darts team had just arrived back from an away game and were having a coffee upstairs while they waited for the snow storm to reduce.

With the dog still between us, I asked if they would like to come and have a look around. However, the dog didn't appear to have the same thoughts and growled as they moved to come in, at which the policemen declined my invitation and backed out the door. Once they'd left, I locked both bar doors and the rest of us sat in the public bar for over an hour after they'd gone.

This was the only time in three years we were visited by the police. I wonder if they were lost or perhaps just cold and wanted a hot coffee on a very cold night.

The Arrogant White Settler

I remember well a regular customer in one of our pubs. He was an elegant man in his late sixties called Charles, and he had a drink problem. He visited the pub in the morning and his regular order would be a Pils lager with three measures of vodka in it. We had to pour it in the other bar and bring it through to the lounge so no one could see what he was drinking, but of course, nearly everyone knew.

Charles was not aristocratic, but wished he was. He was always immaculately dressed and, most of the time, he was polite, friendly and interesting. However, after a few drinks, he could be a little obnoxious. He was reasonably well off and drove the most expensive Ford convertible of the day, which was always garaged by 4pm.

The village itself had three communities: the locals, born and bred in the village; the academics, who worked in the university; and the 'white settlers' from the cities who'd come to the country to live, mainly in the small, new private housing estate. The groups generally didn't mix, although they knew each other. On occasions, they spoke to each other but only if there was no one else from their group about. Charles was different; he regarded and referred to the locals as peasants and they regarded him as an aloof, snobby drunk.

It was Saturday lunchtime and Charles was in the lounge for his usual four Pils specials and holding court to the lunching tourists. Outside, the earlier sunshine had been replaced by a heavy shower. In the public bar, the villagers were enjoying their Saturday lunchtime drink, debating the afternoon's possible football results, while looking through the window at Charles's convertible slowly filling with rain water. No one was going to tell him that he'd left the hood down and they were just waiting for him to find out.

Like most summer rainstorms, it soon passed over and the sun came out to dry the car park. At this point, Charles, having bored the tourists to distraction, left the lounge and walked out to his car.

It took him a minute to find the keys and the keyhole to start the engine. Once started, he put the car into reverse to move out of his parking space. He must then have realised that he was sitting in a puddle of water, for his car shot backwards across the deserted car park, to where the telephone line men had fenced off an open manhole.

I heard the crash, or rather a loud bump, as one of his rear wheels went down the hole and the front of his car shot up into the air.

I heard the rush of feet as the public bar emptied to see what had happened. I followed to see his car at the far side of the car park, with one wheel in the hole and the front of the car at rather an acute angle. Many stood there laughing as he tried to open the door and get out of the car. He crawled out then slipped in what must have been the only puddle left in the car park, and landed face down in the mud, ruining his light linen suit.

It was only then that the bystanders stopped laughing, helped him to his feet and offered to get his car out of the hole. I brought him into the pub and phoned his wife to come and collect him.

Some villagers towed his car out and parked it, roof down, in the corner of the car park, just as the telephone line men returned to fill in the hole. The following Saturday morning, Charles walked into the public bar and bought all the locals a drink for helping him out the week before.

Interesting how this incident changed the relationship between the three village communities. Charles became known to the locals as 'the likeable village posh drunk', he called them 'the lads', and he would often join them in the bar on a Saturday and buy the drinks.

Charles's Dog Walk

One of Charles's passions was to walk round the village immaculately dressed, as was his little white West Highland terrier called Herbert. He and his wife would often pop in with the dog to show me a new coat they'd bought him, or just to show him off. I remember the day he came in to show me his new retractable lead, explaining that it would allow the dog to run round in the field without escaping, or him having to chase it.

A couple of days later, on an early winter's evening, dark and crisp but pleasant for a stroll, Charles was taking Herbert for a walk down the dimly lit high street. Being after 6pm, Charles was, perhaps, a little inebriated.

I heard a screech of brakes and looked out of the window to see a dog on the other side of the road, whining. Thinking the dog had been hit, I rushed out. I found Charles sitting on the ground outside the pub front door, dazed and shouting for Herbert. A car had stopped in the middle of the road with lights flashing, and the dog was whining on the other side of the car.

I quickly checked the driver, who was okay, then went over to the dog. He was still on his lead but it was caught on the car, so I unclipped the lead from him and carried him over to Charles, who was by now complaining of pain in his wrist.

A couple of minutes later, Charles was sitting in the pub, without a drink, waiting for the doctor to come and see him, while his wife soothed the distressed Herbert, who appeared more shocked than hurt. After the driver left with nothing more than a fright, Charles proceeded to tell his wife and me what had happened.

Charles had been walking the dog along the pavement, turned right into the high street, and crossed the road to walk down the left hand side, while the dog, on his lovely extendable lead, had followed the wall and, taking the sharp turn, had walked down the right hand side of the road.

Charles and the dog were now on opposite sides of the road when a car, not seeing the slim lead attached to both dog and man, had driven into it, jerking both of them off their feet, before tearing the lead from Charles's hand.

Charles had broken his wrist and was in plaster for several weeks. Needless to say, the lead was never used again.

The Late Night Barman

Like most publicans we had a dog. In fact at times we had lots of dogs, and this is one of the many stories of Cleo, a large blue Great Dane bitch.

Cleo had a large outside kennel with a run for during the day, but in the evening, she would be upstairs above the pub guarding our personal accommodation. At closing time, she would wander down the stairs, crash open the door at the bottom, and calmly saunter across the room to sit down by the bar hatch, where she would stay waiting for everyone to leave. Once all the customers had left, she would saunter over and lie in front of the fire, until either my wife or I let her out to her run.

It was one Monday evening, and my wife and I had gone out to dinner, leaving the pub in the hands of our very competent barman, Bill, Timmy the chef in the kitchen, and Gill the resident nanny upstairs looking after the children.

After an excellent dinner, we met up with friends, who invited us back to their house for coffee. It was just after 1.30am when we arrived back in the pub car park. The first unusual thing we noticed was the bar lights were still on, and, as we approached the entrance, Cleo began barking on the other side of the door.

We entered to find Bill sitting behind the bar enjoying a beer, with the bar hatch locked. He explained that Cleo, who had always been soft with him, had decided the bar was closed and no one should be in it, including Bill. Every time he tried to leave, she growled and barked at him, so he reckoned he would just have a lock-in on his own.

I asked why Gill hadn't come down and let him out. He said that he'd called her on the intercom several times but got no response. We checked and found her upstairs in bed, sound asleep and far away from the bar intercom.

Bill did offer to pay for the two pints and two whiskies he'd had while waiting for us to return, but instead he and I had another drink with the dog.

During all the time we had Cleo, she was extremely protective of the bar areas once customers had left, and we had to be careful not to leave her there out of opening hours if there were people working in the public areas. Throughout her life, she always entered the bar at closing time and peacefully emptied the bar.

You're Barred

It's funny how sometimes you get your own back in ways you never expected. We bought a village pub, which for many years had been known as a good food pub, but in the year prior to us taking over, it had a new owner. He'd changed the menu completely and turned it into 'a sausage pub'. In less than a year of ownership, he'd lost all the previous custom for traditional meals successfully built up over ten years. The pub was almost dead. We decided to oust the sausages and return to steaks, roasts, fresh fish, home cooked soups and desserts.

It was a spring Sunday lunchtime, just a couple of months after taking over the pub. Business was now returning. I was standing behind the bar looking down across the lounge to the front door, when in walked a well-dressed, rather portly man with his family. From the door, he shouted across to me, "Ah landlord, a table for five and bring the sausage menu over," then proceeded to sit at a table clearly marked 'reserved'.

The voice triggered something in my memory and, as I walked over to the table, it came to me: SCHOOL. This was the little s**t who had me caned for putting a pair of trousers on the top of the school flagpole. At the time, he said he had seen me and two others shinnying up the pole.

Well, I hadn't. In fact, I'd taken the afternoon off (truancy, they call it) to go down to the river and spend the afternoon on the ferry. As I couldn't say where I was, or who I was with, I took the cane but vowed to get him back, and now was my chance, a mere seventeen years later.

On reaching the table, I tapped him on the shoulder and, in a voice loud enough for everyone in the pub to hear, I said, “I told you last time, you’re barred, now take your brats and leave and I never want to see you in here again!”

He jumped up and turned round, his face now very red, and said, “I think you must have mistaken me for someone else. I’ve never been in this establishment before.” I replied, “You’re George Brown and this is your other wife, is it?” to which he stammered, “Ye, ye, yes, no, no it’s my only wife!” “I really don’t care which of your women you try to bring in here after the last time, now you’re barred so get out!” I demanded.

I watched them leave, with him trying to explain to his wife that he’d never been in the pub before, and her angrily asking why I knew his name. Sweet revenge made even sweeter by the fact that he didn’t even know who I was.

Where has all the water gone?

Some years ago, we purchased a fifteen-bedroom hotel on the outskirts of Edinburgh, which had operated for a number of years as a lounge bar, with bed and breakfast, supplemented by the odd small function. Our intention was to bring it up to AA three star standards within a couple of years.

This would require a programme of improvements, including new boilers to cope with the heating and hot water, a new kitchen, the redecoration of public areas and bedrooms, as well as the removal of all the junk from the outbuilding. An interesting fact is in the first month we had enough junk to fill seven skips and a lorry with reinforced steel girders.

We decided to keep open the large lounge bar with its separate entrance and facilities, while the renovation work was being done. We had just completed fitting the new kitchen and the public areas, when we received a request from the Royal Air Force (RAF) balloon team for twelve lads to stay in the hotel for a week.

This had the possibility of being a regular reservation, so I was anxious to accept the booking. I explained we were still undertaking improvements but this shouldn't affect their stay. They accepted the reservation and arrived two days later on the Sunday evening and left early for work on Monday.

On the Monday, the weather started off with mist and rain, making it unsuitable for jumping. However by late morning, the poor weather cleared, enabling the guys to do one parachute jump, before a downpour at about three o'clock stopped their activities for the day and they returned to the hotel.

They arrived back soaking wet and cold saying they were all going up for a quick bath before coming down to the bar for a drink. I returned from reception and went back to serving the few early evening customers in the cocktail bar. A couple of minutes later, the bell at reception rang and I went out to find one of the RAF guys wrapped in a towel, wanting to know where the hot water had gone.

"Gone?" I stammered. "Yes, gone," he said. "I turned on the hot water, went back to the bedroom, took my clothes off and when I went back, the tap was still turned on but there was no water coming out of it." Just then a couple of the other lads, also wrapped in towels, appeared on the staircase, shouting across that their hot water had disappeared as well. Somewhat confused and thinking we must have a leak, I rushed upstairs to investigate.

I knocked on the first door. No reply, so I opened the door with my master key and, hearing someone in the bath, I shouted through the door to check all was well, no leaks and that he had hot water. "Yes," came the reply though the door.

I apologised and went next door to the room of one of the gentlemen waiting at reception. On entering the bathroom, I found the hot water running into the bath, I turned the tap off and went down to tell him his bath was running. I then went up to the next room to find no hot water coming out of the open tap.

Confused, I turned the tap off and went back down to the guys asking if they all had the same difficulty. It appeared they all had the same problem, no water coming out of the taps, so I went back up to each of their rooms and turned off their hot water taps in case the water suddenly returned. On my return, the guys had moved from the front hall reception and were now sitting in the bar having a drink, still dressed in their towels. It did look strange.

Now totally confused, I asked if I could go back to their rooms and investigate further. I went back to room three and turned on the hot water and, hey presto, it worked. I turned off the tap and went to room four and again it worked, as did all the remaining rooms.

I was now totally baffled, one minute hot water, the next none. My mind said there was a blockage somewhere so I phoned the plumber, who was going to be installing the new boiler later in the month, and asked him to come and have a look. Then back to the bar to tell the guys the hot water was working. They finished their drinks and went up to their rooms to bathe.

A couple of minutes later, two of the five returned, still no hot water. I was totally perplexed when through the front door came the plumber. He said, "I think I know what the problem is. Could you ask the guys to have a ten minute interval between each bath and it should be OK." So they drew lots to determine their bathing order and off they went, either back to the bar or their rooms, and, yes, they all got hot water in the end.

The next morning, the plumber arrived early and explained that the previous owner had added ten bathrooms without changing the original feed pipes designed to deliver sufficient water to only two bathrooms. When I asked why we hadn't had the problem earlier, he said, "Probably pure luck, not everyone had a bath at the same time."

Well, for the rest of their stay, the lads took turns and, a couple of weeks later, the plumber fitted the new hot and cold water supply pipes, and replaced the baths with showers, which use less water.

But every time the team came to stay, the request was always the same, "Could I have room one please, the one with the permanent hot water supply?"

Leftovers

My elder daughter, Clare, a chirpy, chatty little girl who'd been brought up in the hotel, was almost six years old when this event occurred.

It was our first parents' evening. We were going to see our precious little daughter's teacher, Miss Clark, to find out how our Clare was getting on at school. The meeting started well and we puffed with pride as she told us Clare was a lovely, lively girl, well liked and progressing well.

As we were about to leave, Miss Clark told us she had been dying to tell us how she found out we were hoteliers.

"It was a few weeks ago, during a communication lesson on a Monday morning. I asked each child to stand up and describe to the class what they had for Sunday lunch. Well, Clare, having a surname at the end of the alphabet, was the last to speak, as usual. We had listened to a range of Sunday meals, normally a roast, but some were a bit different and some went out to a restaurant. Then Clare stood up and looked round the room before saying:

'On Sundays, we sit down for lunch at three o'clock in the afternoon and eat the leftovers.'

"There was a gasp from the other children and I quickly intervened by asking Clare what she meant by leftovers. To which she replied, 'Whatever food is left over.' Somewhat shocked, I interrupted once again, "Left over from where?" Clare looked at me and with disdain said, "The restaurant, of course."

"Oh," I said. "What do you eat then?" Quite confused, she said, "We have roast beef, lamb, fillet steak or Dover soles, which I don't like, but whatever is left over from the restaurant Sunday lunch service."

I have to say both my daughters are clearly foodies, for today they remember occasions by the menu, quality of the food and the level of service.

Overbooked at Christmas

Throughout my time in the hotel industry, I often observed staff working beyond the expectations of their jobs to ensure customers were not disappointed. There's definitely something in the saying 'giving satisfaction is satisfying'. It's to all of those staff who go that one step beyond expectations I write this tale, especially poignant because of when it happened.

It was Christmas Eve in London, freezing cold and raining hard. I was the only unmarried member of the management team and therefore duty manager over the festive holiday. The hotel accommodation was fully booked, although the banqueting suites were empty and the restaurants now closed. As midnight approached, a young family arrived at reception to check in. They'd booked their accommodation some weeks earlier. It was for one night, before they would head off for a family gathering on Christmas Day.

Unfortunately, they hadn't read the hotel's confirmation letter, which clearly stated in large bold letters, 'Arrival must be before 6pm, after which time the booking will be released unless fully paid in advance'. Regrettably, their room had been released, and to make matters worse, the hotel was fully booked.

I met them at reception and explained that at 9.30pm, assuming they were not going to arrive, we'd released their booking as they hadn't pre-paid or arrived before 6.00pm. As normal in such circumstances, I phoned every hotel in the area to try and find a room for them but without success. There was no accommodation available anywhere nearby on this Christmas Eve.

By now the two young children were crying. To cheer them up, the head night porter brought a complimentary tray of cakes, milk and tea. It was about then that Jamie, one of the night porters, came up with an idea. "We have four small portable beds, sir, don't we?" he asked, to which I nodded, and he said, "Right, sir, give us ten minutes and we'll sort something out." I sat down with the family while the porters went off to arrange some accommodation. At the time, I remember thinking it couldn't be a staff flat as I knew they were all full. Anyway, about ten minutes later, the night porters returned, all smiles. "All sorted, sir," said Jamie. The family and I followed them up to the banqueting reception area and into the ladies' powder room. They'd covered the floor with Santa's grotto rug, set up four beds, fitted a bolt lock to the inside of the door and placed a large card on the outside of the door. It read 'CLOSED FOR REPAIRS'. Most astonishingly, they'd put up some Christmas decorations. It looked fantastic and the kids just loved it. I can honestly say I've seldom seen a family so happy with their accommodation, even if it did have four toilets and wash basins.

It was a Christmas they and our night staff would never forget. I went to check on them during breakfast and the children told me Santa had left two small Christmas stockings, filled with fruit and sweets, pinned on the door for them. The parents paid for their family room and, before leaving, left a note of thanks for the night staff.

The next evening, I gave the night staff the note and they were so pleased to have helped this family in distress on Christmas Eve. Finally, the family sent a note to the company chairman praising the hotel staff for making their Christmas one to remember instead of one to forget.

No, we didn't nickname the night porters the three wise men, and a loo is definitely much better than a stable on a wet, cold night.

A Garden Party

My final story in this selection occurred while I was managing a very beautiful Garden Hotel. It was early spring and the weather had been sunny and dry for the last few days. As I arrived back to my office, I was met by a very enthusiastic young assistant manager, just dying to tell me something important.

I sat and listened as he told me, "I've just taken a booking on the phone for next Thursday, 250 mainly vegetarians wanting a late breakfast at ten-thirty. I quoted them the full price plus 25% and they've agreed."

"Anything else?" I asked.

"They asked about our gardens and would it be possible to meet up on the lawn. I told them we have a lovely lawn and, weather permitting that would be no problem."

As he got up to leave and make the arrangements, I asked, "Who's the booking for?"

"A Miss Geraldine Raff," he replied.

"Was it a company booking or private?" I questioned.

"I'm not sure," he replied, "but I did get her phone number and address."

"Can you please give her a ring and check?" and he left to ring her.

Five minutes later, he returned. "You knew, didn't you? I asked for Miss Geraldine Raff and the man said, 'Not another one who wants to speak to the giraffe'. It was Bristol Zoo and you knew."

"Yes," I said, "it was when I noticed next Thursday is April the first, and before you go, don't take any bookings for the swimming pool next week for a Mr Charles Lyon either."

I didn't tell the staff but by lunchtime, they must have all known because the chef asked him if he wanted a plate of grass for his important customer.

Back Page

I started work in the hospitality industry before we had computers and still had pounds, shillings and pence; an exciting time of economic, social and technological change, with the hospitality industry undergoing great expansion and development.

There was growing prosperity; people were beginning to have more discretionary income to spend on leisure; eating out in restaurants, taking holidays overseas and mini breaks in UK city hotels.

This expansion offered me employment in many hospitality establishments; starting as a trainee and working in various positions before owning my own hotel, village inn and guesthouse.

On leaving the hospitality industry I spent the rest of my working life in Further Education, training young people to be ready and suitably skilled for employment and latterly specialising in liaising with employers, supporting personnel development and improving business processes.

Since retiring, I have continued my love of sailing; circumventing Great Britain and undertaking a number of voyages, while volunteering with Princes Trust and The National Coastwatch Institution.

I would like to express my thanks and acknowledge those wonderful people who have helped in compiling the book: Christine Holland, Anne Gibb and Ken McKenzie for reading and editing many of the stories, with very special thanks for a young talented artist Faye Thirtle for the illustrations.

Finally, my life would not be complete without my family; wife, daughters, the grandsons and new granddaughter.

Useful Links

Illustrations: Faye Thirtle
www.artistsandillustrators.co.uk/fayehobsonillustration

Brian Wilson
www.alexanderbrianwilson.com